LOVE2Heal

A Science 2 Soul Perspective to understand how your Body is Seeking Reconnection Through the Language of Pain and Dis-ease

Healing our Mind and Body through the E-Motion of LOVE

Listen- Observe-Visualise-Empower.

Gemma Louisa

Copyright © 2024 Gemma Louisa

The Infinity Health Hub Limited

All rights reserved.

ISBN: 9798346223535

DEDICATION

This is a dedication to Zachary and Olly, my two beautiful children, who without them, I would not have understood unconditional love the way I do.
For them, I strive to be the better version of myself every day. To become a more conscious parent and to break the patterns of generations, so they too can live a life in their truth, health and happiness.

CONTENTS

	Acknowledgments	i
1	Preface	1
2	LOVE2HEAL	3
3	How did 2020 serve and challenge me	7
4	Self-Reflection – Wheel of Life	13
5	Our Sacred Plan – Our Path of Happiness	16
6	Self-Exploration & Reflection Exercises	21
7	Our External Experiences Mirror our Internal World	28
8	Our Body's Tapestry	34
9	Healing Through the E-Motion of Love	37
10	What is Self-Love	41
11	The Pyjama Revolution	47
12	To Breathe or to not to Breathe	49
13	Homeostasis by Breath	58
14	How our Emotions are Reflected within our Body	66
15	How Meditation Affects our Mind	77
16	The Chakras	82
17	Base Chakra	86

18	Sacral Chakra	98
19	Solar Plexus	108
20	Heart Chakra	122
21	Throat Chakra	143
22	Prelude to the Brow and Crown Chakra	165
23	Brow Chakra	168
24	Crown Chakra	172
25	The Bridge of Connection	179
26	The Eyes Tell it All	185
27	Trusting Our Layers of Insight – Our Sixth Sense	190
28	Paradox –Duality as One – Balance	197
29	Finding Our Balance of Rest and Action	208
30	Bindu – The Apex of Connection	211
31	Cerebrospinal Fluid	213
32	The Crown and Sacral Relationship	219
33	What is Your Truth?	222
34	What is Your Frequency?	228
35	Healing is Skin Deep	231
36	The Pineal Gland	236

ACKNOWLEDGMENTS

I wish to say thank you to all of my clients over the years, who trusted in me on their journey of health and wellbeing, without you I would not know what I know today!

My friends, Ria and Michelle that supported me to create LOVE2Heal as a brand, and worked tirelessly to get The Infinity Health Hub and the LOVE2Heal online course looking as great as it does.

To my Mum, Patricia – my chief co-editor, making sure one's grammar was correct, who would have preferred there to be no swear words in this book!

To my husband Ade, who has supported me in my dreams, even when he did not understand them all of the time, however, he believed in me.

To my beautiful pooch, Jess – without her I would not have had as many walks in nature, sea swims, sunsets and sunrises – all moments of connection to Earth and myself. Where I was able to discover this innate wisdom, and parts of self, hidden in my subconscious and unconscious to be healed, alchemised and transformed, all within a place of love and acceptance, the shadow and light.

Lastly, to my Higher Self-my Soul, for guiding one on this journey of transformation through self-love, trust and acceptance. Much of this book comes from my heart and a higher wisdom that comes from within- to the point where I feel one cannot take all the credit!

Quite often through meditation, quiet contemplation and walks, key wisdom would simply "drop in" to my consciousness, as a deeper inner knowing, from which, I would excitingly explore to find the Science of this new "Intel" that could be weaved into our understanding and acceptance.

It has been a journey of perseverance, passion and determination, to get this message of self-empowerment to as many people that I can; which has been the light of navigation through some of the darkest of days, *the Dark Night of the Soul*.

Upon reflection, I now see this as my greatest blessing - I see and embody all of the gold it has shown me.

1.

PREFACE

HEALING OUR MIND AND BODY - THROUGH THE E-MOTION OF LOVE

***L**isten- **O**bserve-**V**isualise-**E**mpower.*

As pain follows the same neural pathways as loneliness – it is my belief through personal and professional experience, that our bodies are the root and compass to our deepest purpose as a Soul – and when we are separated from our power, our love and acceptance of self, through the dis-coherence of Mind –Heart-Body and Soul, we also have become mis-aligned to our joy and purpose – the body will give us sweet messages to guide us back to self – our power our sovereignty – It is up to us to start listening!

Through this book, I hope to start your journey of a deeper sense of awareness of self, to begin to truly recognise the miracle that you are and how worthy you are of love, joy and peace in abundance, which begins with the conscious connection to you, your body!

I share a Science to Soul concept - supported through science to bridge you to find your Soul –your purpose, passion and inner power that has always been within you. To empower you in your health and wellbeing Mind-Body- Heart and Soul, through a deeper sense of awareness, enabling you to make conscious choices of change for yourself and the world around you.

It is a stepping stone in your journey of self-love, acceptance and trust, with your heart as your anchor and navigator.

Sharing my own experiences with guidance and suggested self-care, awareness and self-reflection exercises, which are expanded and embodied through meditation and neural plasticity via the LOVE2Heal 21-day online course.

To support and guide you to feel more grounded and connected to oneself, to feel more empowered in one's own health, to recognise mind and body as one which need your love and care.

2.

LOVE2HEAL

It is my belief that when we hold unconditional love and kindness for ourselves, we become a liberation process of releasing restrictive thoughts, our fears and traumas that constrict our bodies to a cellular level. From my experience and knowledge in this field, I truly believe our unresolved emotional layers form physical restrictions and adhesions of the body through constriction on a cellular level.

Connecting and working with the fascia and somatic system (our skin and nervous system), bridges our internal and external self, our conscious and subconscious mind and our unconscious body. We are able to release restrictions physically, emotionally and mentally, allowing expansion from our cellular level to our whole body existence and presence; gifting ourselves space to breathe, to flow and be comfortable in ourselves and our skin. With this comes an inner peace and joy, neutralising our daily stressors to sustain a healthy body and mind.

This book is designed to connect our physical and emotional self, our internal and external environment and our relationships within both.

My vision is to empower those who wish to improve their health and wellbeing mind and body, through sharing knowledge of the intricate connection of our emotional and physical self, and how our unresolved emotions overtime cause restrictions, dysfunction and later dis-ease - empowering oneself through practicing self-awareness and reflection, self-care techniques and meditation.

My mission, dream and passion is that this will become an introduction and guidance in your journey of establishing and developing a flowing communication of your mind, body, heart and soul - to find your inner truth, power and magick. To be a stepping stone for you to create a pathway of awareness and empowered conscious choices in your daily life, acknowledging that your health and wellbeing is based upon all aspects of your life, from work and purpose, to relationships and the environment that surrounds you.

Through connection and trust, you begin to forge a deeper union of mind and body and your relationship with yourself; to understand what serves you joy and happiness and to be able to recognise and release old restrictive thoughts, beliefs and emotions that no longer serve you purpose on your journey of life.

Through self-love and acceptance, you hold the courage and strength to give yourself the permission to be fully you, unapologetically, and to embody curiosity of what your pure potentiality will feel, and look like, as you constantly evolve and grow.

The concept of LOVE – Listen Observe Visualise Empower has come from my own experiences and with clients, suffering from a range of ailments of musculoskeletal to stress related illnesses, that when we unpeel each layer from the physical, there are emotional undertones restricting on a cellular level.

These emotions are energetic vibrations in our bodies, and ultimately comes down to how much we love and accept ourselves, and the frequencies we are resonating in emotionally, consciously or subconsciously; be they of constrictive low vibrational fear, anger, shame, guilt or the open and expansive high energy of gratitude, love and joy and, later peace and calm,

Through holding pure unconditional love for ourselves, where we are not swayed by criticism or praise, to know that you are enough, releases the foot off the pedal and the undue stress we place upon ourselves and our bodies in our day to day lives.

To heal through the open and expansive emotion of love and by practicing daily, the mantra of LOVE - **L**isten and **O**bserve your body, understanding what it is trying to tell you through pain, discomfort and illness, to **V**isualise space and healing opening new neural pathways through affirmations, intentions and movement meditation, to **E**mpower yourself, owning your health and wellbeing mind and body.

To form an understanding as to how our bodies physically reflect our emotions and thoughts, and begin to form a supportive foundation through affirmations and self-awareness, to become the observer of one's mind and body, and to recognise your body's tapestry, to be able to read your body, your physical self, and how it is reflecting your inner self, your mind and the deep rooted thoughts, emotions, beliefs and fears.

LOVE2Heal online course

To reinforce your learning and health empowerment you can purchase the LOVE2Heal 21 day course via The Infinity Health Hub, to go deeper within, to self-reflect, releasing yourself from un-serving patterns and beliefs with structured workbooks and guided meditations for each chakra.

It is designed to support you in developing greater awareness and love for self, transmuting in a healthier and happier mind, body, heart and soul.

The guided freestyle movement mediations within the LOVE2Heal course support you to breathe, to connect and bridge your mind, heart and body's relationship. To truly hear, feel and love your body and tap into the instinctive ways of movement, to open and find physical space within your miraculous body, and allow the release of physical tensions and emotions that no longer serves you.

Forging a deeper union of mind and body and your relationship with yourself; to understand what serves you joy, love, contentment and fulfillment, and to be able to recognise and release old restrictive thoughts, beliefs and emotions that no longer serve you purpose on your journey of health and happiness.

I envisage this book and the online course will become an introduction and guidance in your journey of establishing and developing the connection of your mind, heart, body and soul, with the intention to guide you on your path of wholeness, health and happiness.

Use the voucher code IAMENOUGH to get 15% off as a gift and thank you from me.

Love You Gemma

https://www.theinfinityhealthhub.com/courses/love2heal

3.

2020 – HOW DID IT SERVE AND CHALLENGE ME?

2020-2021 was a challenging year for many people on many levels, physically and emotionally. Our health became the paramount issue and focus individually, collectively and globally. Our health has probably never been in the forefront of our minds as it has been before, however, unfortunately information about how we are responsible and how to be empowered through knowledge about one's health hasn't been as widely broadcasted.

2020 challenged me to reflect and look within. The medium of zoom accentuated this, as I physically had to look at myself, which was most uncomfortable at first; it triggered my insecurities, as being at ease and at peace within my body has always been a challenge for me, especially since my teenage years.

Gradually I have become more at ease seeing me and knowing that others see me and that is okay, my inner judgemental self has quietened, and I hold more love and kindness for myself, which is intrinsic for our health and wellbeing mind and body. Now I can't help but be distracted by looking at myself, which is pretty amusing!

I found myself guiding through thoughts, emotions, fears and belief systems which in some form, have always restricted me from being my true potential and fulfilling my purpose throughout my life. I was recognising and acknowledging what no longer served my purpose, and what I needed to let go of, if I wanted to grow and evolve. I felt like I was teasing myself out of a chrysalis, my restricted safety, yet I was beginning to see life more creatively, opening myself to greater opportunities and learning to trust these new beginnings and believe in myself.

When we recognise that these various restrictive thought and trigger patterns, old belief systems and the various levels of fear, serve us neither joy, or purpose; for our precious time on this wonderful planet and their detrimental effect on our health mind and body. We have the choice to set the intention not to be restricted with these thoughts, and to hold more joy and love, and to live more within the present moment, the moment that we are only guaranteed.

Setting the intention to release un-serving emotions and fears and to hold more joy and love within our mind and body, we begin to open one's heart to hold unconditional love and the first person you must begin to love is YOU! To hold kindness and love unconditionally for oneself, liberated and free from restrictive bonds and cords, we become a creative and expansive energy, co-creating ones dreams. Tapping into the abundant frequency of love and joy, is part of the healing process, it expands our bodies on a cellular level, opening the cells to release, to function, and to absorb the light of our being and the substance of life itself, oxygen.

One element of fear, is the fear of the unknown, this experience has highlighted control, how much control we humans wish to have. Ultimately we are simply only in control of our perceptions, our emotions and our actions, the rest is up to the universe and the collective of individuals, as we are all interlinked more than we realise. Surrendering what one cannot control is a huge leap of faith and trust that we will be supported, even when we don't know how!

My own personal experience raised fear of the unknown, how

would I be financially supported through this is if I couldn't work in my clinic? At this point I turned to running and deepened my meditation practice to help me ride this rollercoaster. Through meditation it gave me the space for my thoughts and to release from fears, to open my mind to allow more creative thoughts and welcome new opportunities.

Whilst meditating within groups via zoom, the individuals would come to me, like a hologram in Star Wars and I would visualise placing my hands on their head to read the body, (which I physically do in my clinics).

What followed was a light trail within their body which highlighted the areas in their body that needed healing and I proceeded to visualise working their body as I would physically, yet the body was more energetic and fluid and I could see the internal nerves, arteries, which I'm familiar with from studying the human anatomy.

Undeniably this blew me away, and yes the voice of "ego" came in to tell me I couldn't have seen this, this isn't possible, right, I simply have an active mind?! So I continued to experiment "safely" on friends and family, who I knew wouldn't laugh at me for being ridiculous.... Welcome to my fear of rejection raising its voice.

One of these experiences was with a friend who had just had a cycling accident, he had fallen onto his side and his hips really hurt, he felt he was walking in circles! So we had a call, and I tuned in, and it brought up emotions about his parents within his hips, which we had a chat about, I didn't do any intentional distance healing at that time. The next day I have a message to say he can walk perfectly fine and the pain had gone! – This perplexed us both! How could a very obvious physical injury which you can pin-point to, actually be healed through the emotional aspect that had been brought to the surface from the accident- was the accident actually an accident, as in some way the Universe instigated the incident to bring the emotions to be processed, and healed - or did the emotions create the incident?!

This truly challenges how we see ourselves and life, our bodies as flesh and bone, as dense physical matter - as the great man Einstein said, "*Concerning matter, we have been all wrong. What we have called matter is energy, whose vibration has been so lowered as to be perceptible to the senses. There is no matter*".

Through confirmation of these experiences and continuing my meditation practice, the message was to offer this as a new service. Well now my voice of fear of rejection, and not being good enough is screaming, trying to protect me it says, as this or I, could be seen as Mumbo Jumbo!!

However, with the meditations I visualised a huge circle of light right in front of me, making what felt like the centre of my brow expanding. It felt filled with love and acceptance, and I was to step into this light even though I did not know what I was stepping into. It was a matter of faith and trust that I would be supported, that I was enough!

Skipping ahead a few months, from trusting the unknown and initiating the process of releasing from fear, I found myself more enlightened about the mind-body-core intrinsic relationship, and looking at my business with a creative mind, filling with many other opportunities.

It was clear, that to heal people, one needs to support them to be able to form a bridge, connecting their mind and body through the power of breath, to release the constrains of the mind and thoughts and to flow within. To feel and listen to their entire body, empowering to self-heal, which in itself is liberating and healing to know you have an active part in your health and wellbeing.

Thus believing my role as a therapist is to be a bridge of trust, holding a safe loving space filled with acceptance, compassion and non-judgement for clients to understand and acknowledge, what their body is trying to tell them and to share self-care techniques to start the process of healing.

"To be able to heal others is a great and wonderful gift,

To be able to enlighten and empower others to heal themselves is even greater"

Through understanding this level of healing, I began to write. Drawing my knowledge together on all plains, from the science of the physical therapy, the quantum physics of energetic healing, how emotions underlay our physical state and how these cross over with the chakra systems energetically, emotionally and physically.

My intention is to put all this information in one place, where people can understand what their body is trying to tell them. To show how to connect their mind and body, and how to physically support their body, becoming enlightened and empowered for their own health and being.

Several months later, again I found the online consultations with guided meditation evolved into holding group meditations which then opened into the corporate world of wellbeing. If I am honest, I had not detailed in my vision of growth, these outcomes; I had simply asked to have the confidence to grow, to come out of the shadows and to share my knowledge to help others.

It is amazing when you release and trust that you will be supported and remove the constraints of thoughts, old beliefs and fears, and tune into love and joy as your frequency. My manifestation of coming out of the shadows, to be supported financially materialised, in ways I had not believed possible.

When one releases un-serving old thought patterns, belief systems and emotions, and visualise ourselves in this joyful and supported existence, without the minute details, and have an open and creative mind to all opportunities, believing that one deserves abundance, then it flows to us naturally in ways one cannot imagine.

It is my wish and hope that from picking up this book and/or doing the course, you are ready to empower yourself to heal internally and externally, to connect your mind and body. To understand how our inner and deep rooted emotions affect our health, relationships and our world individually and collectively. To acknowledge that you are a co-creator of your world on your path to find purpose, contentment, health and true happiness.

Sending so much love and support

Open Our Hearts

4.

SELF-REFLECTION - THE WHEEL OF LIFE

"I am now creating my success, in an easy and relaxed manner, in a healthy and positive way"

"I have all the support of the universe to achieve my hearts desires with abundance"

"I am co-creating the world I wish it to be"

This book through self-explorative work, breathing techniques, gentle exercises, affirmations, has been created to help you to open your mind, body and soul, to connect to your true heart desires, forming a healthy empowerment.

To feel supported and secure, establishing strong foundations and roots, allowing your creativity to evolve and grow, to hold self-acceptance and belief in one-self, to know that "You Are Enough".

To simply be you, to hold love and kindness within your heart for oneself, enabling you to speak with strength, honesty and integrity of your heart desires; to visualise this life of abundance that you wish to create; to form a more peripheral vision open to receiving guidance and pathways of opportunities beyond your initial thoughts, and to trust that you will be supported.

Liberate the anchor of "the restraining known" and expand the sails to explore through the ocean of opportunities.

Finding time and space for ourselves is imperative for our

wellbeing mind and body. To carve out time within our daily lives to step off the "rapidly moving conveyor belt of life"," the spin of the hamster wheel"; to enable ourselves to become grounded and centred, to tune into our thoughts and to recognise when we are out-of-balance and to simply breathe.

Our breath is the bridge between the intrinsic relationship of our mind and body. Relaxed deep breaths slow down our minds, enabling ourselves to feel rather than think, connecting our thoughts and emotions and how they are held within a miracle itself, our bodies. Our body is a tapestry reflecting our minds, calling upon us to look within and hold love for ourselves when those niggles, pains, dis-eases surface.

Deep abdominal breathing taps into and opens the connection to our second brain, the gut-brain, which holds an imprint of our whole body within. It is reading our relationship and interaction with the environment around us, it stores unresolved emotions that the conscious brain cannot sustain, it is our "knowing" and "feeling" whether something is right or wrong for us, "our gut instinct".

Through breath we unite with our feelings, releasing old restrictive thought patterns, images, emotions and traumas, which have become the matrix of our bodies and mind, which no longer serve us purpose.

Our upbringing and social environment impacts us as to how safe and secure one feels, how supported, loved and to hold a sense of belonging in this world. It shapes, moulds and drives us through a "social tunnel of expectations" as to what we feel we *should*, *have* and *need* to be within this world.

This "social tunnel" is our illusion of security, our sense of control, the belief that should one do what is expected, one will be supported and accepted into this world, however, challenging oneself to look within and see if it truly represents our deepest heart desires?

Ingrained for many, is a belief system, a thought process that following one's heart desires, the creative element of one's being would not be supported, and hence one *should/have/need* to seek a more "secure" and "stable" career/path.

Each one of us has a purpose and a gift, a gift to enhance this world both individually and collectively. This gift arises in many forms, be they grounding, balanced and supportive; expressive with creativity and joy; strength and inspirational; loving and healing; speaks with authenticity and integrity; insightful, inspirational and open minded. These individual gifts accumulate, interweave and interlace in roles as a teacher, a leader, a supporter, a healer, a carer, a creator, an inventor, an evolutionary, a visionary.

Finding our true self, establishing our gift within this world we become fulfilled we have a purpose. Life becomes meaningful, naturally raising our emotional level to hold more positive feelings of joy, and feeling part of this world, that we belong.

This higher resonance and frequency of emotions fundamentally improves our mind and body, health and wellbeing. Tapping into this energetic field, the source of our being, this energetic wave of abundance enables us to be empowered, to become a co-creator of our true heart desires and dreams, influencing the world around us.

"My Presence in this World is a Gift"

5.

OUR SACRED PLAN – OUR PATH OF HAPPINESS

"Deeds done in harmony with one's path of life

are those which bring clarity and peace and harmony to the doer."

Sayings of the Buddha

Have you ever found yourself asking, "What is this all about, what is the purpose of life?"

Have you ever wondered why such energy behind creating a beautiful and miraculous being that has taken thousands of years to evolve is to simply survive, go through heartache, work hard, reproduce then die? Surely there is more a purpose to all this energy that is used to create us wonderful beings?

Maybe that is the way, however, to me it seems like an awful waste of time and energy and a miracle, for that to be all there is in life.

Are we to be like ants soldiering on, or busy bees working hard…*just keep going…just keep going*? (*Actually, this is more like Dory from Finding Nemo!*) However, when we seek objectively, seeing the whole picture of our individual and collective purpose to this world, we all have a part to play, a purpose to sustain this planet, Mother Earth.

So what is our purpose on this planet, are we a necessary part of the ecosystem, would it survive without us? To me the answer is an undisputable YES! Mother Earth has survived for millions of years, her creatures evolving and balancing the ecosystem. Which leads us beautifully to The Big Question, why are we here, why are we these miraculous beings on this beautiful planet, and what is our purpose?

Our human being self is about survival, existing, reproducing, the cycle of life, yet simply existing to me is not overly fulfilling, and maybe our soul's purpose of us being, is to find our happiness, the Dharma, the Sanskrit for "the right way of living".

If happiness is our soul's purpose, how do we achieve this individually? Is there a limit of happiness out there that we need to race to, to be the first to ensure our own happiness? Or is it a path we journey through collectively, supporting one another to each find our happiness and purpose? Can one person be happy solely on their own, as we are genetically social beings?

Considering that we need the simplicity of touch from another, which improves our health and wellbeing; I would surmise it would be a short-lived empty happiness, if at all!

I saw this image of a hallway filled with balloons and text on social media which puts this quite simply.

A professor gave a balloon to every student, who had to inflate it, write their name on it and throw it in the hallway. The professor then mixes all the balloons. The students were given 5 minutes to find their own balloon. Despite a hectic search, no one found their balloon. At that point the professor told the students to take the first balloon they found and hand it to the person whose name was written on it. Within 5 minutes everyone had their balloon.

The professor then said "these balloons are like happiness, we will never find ours if only looking for our own, however if we care about other people's happiness we will find ours too.

Think of the glow of emotion in your heart when you do something kind for another, a good deed for a stranger, does it not light you up inside? This is joy raising your frequency, your being, opening to the energetic wave of abundance of opportunities and a state of healing.

When we seek to look objectively, from the periphery at our lives, are we able to see our higher purpose for our existence on this amazing planet? For inside every one of us holds an individual gift that is precious, to be shared within this world to collectively support one another, through this existence with love and compassion.

These gifts come in many forms nor limited to; as a teacher of wisdom and creative minds, the loving parent and guardian building the foundations upon which our young souls grow, an inspirational leader and warrior of honesty and integrity, a supporter the foundations of society, a healer supporting others through their journey of pain, physically and emotionally; a carer for the vulnerable, the planet and our animals; a creator of joy and expression; a cultivator; an evolutionary, challenging society's perspective; an inventor; a visionary. All with equal standing and importance," *the collective supports the individual and the individual supports the collective.*

To uncover this invaluable gift already within us, one needs to hold a loving kind space, with self-acceptance for oneself, unbounded from the restrictive ego of fears and doubts, which constrain us from achieving our true dreams, desires and purpose.

What ignites your enthusiasm, lighting you up when you think and talk about it, a passion within? A simple knowing, it comes naturally without having to work or think hard, you feel at ease within yourself, there is a reassurance, it is simply you, feeling peaceful and at one with oneself, often feels like a calling, a piece of oneself.

What would be a Rainbow if it were only a few colours?

Our society has become favorable to boxes and labeling, yet we are all individual and unique. Our fingerprints prove this, there is no one thing that suits all, this is what makes us beautiful and special on this planet. Rather than adjusting and trying to fit in, squeezing for "social acceptance", find your fire and self-acceptance and carve out your own unique space, your voice and expression, knowing that when one is true and honest with love and compassion, there is always a place in this world where you belong.

You do not need to prove yourself to others nor yourself in illusionary achievements of finance, career, and status etc. -YOU ARE ENOUGH just the way you are, at this very moment!

Our society and world is craving for the spectrum of light we all behold – being "on the spectrum" is both creative and beautiful as it challenges the status quo. It challenges society that has been created for the select few and calls the expansion and coherence of mind and heart, to be the catalyst for the evolution of humanity!

It is upon self-love, trust and acceptance that we embody a true sense of belonging that can never be filled by another – we feel safe in oneself and our uniqueness and move from survival to thriving – a joy that lifts us to serve in a way that serves our joy, becoming an infinite return of high frequency energy –this is when we shine our light so bloody bright and step into heartfelt purpose, our own USP (Unique Soul Purpose)!

Our purpose and path of happiness is to make a positive difference in this world, supporting one another with love, kindness and compassion. This can start from simply showing our beautiful smiles to one another; imagine the infectious ripple effect this could have, lifting each other's vibrations.

"I have all the support of the universe to achieve my heart desires with abundance"

"I am grateful to serve a purpose in this world that serves my joy and contentment"

6.

SELF-EXPLORATION & REFLECTION EXERCISES

Now is a Gift, that is why is called the Present.
"My Presence in this World is a Gift"

To help and support you through this exercise of self-exploration and reflection, carve out sometime and a place where you will not be disturbed. Allow this time to be a gentle, non-judgemental and loving space for your inner thoughts and feelings, to be able to look within, with honesty to self-reflect on all aspects of one's life

Throughout the book it would be ideal to journal your thoughts, your emotions and any realisations that occur, any physical and visceral discomforts that present themselves to you.

Writing things down, helps us to extract the thoughts that swirl around in our minds into something physical that we can read back to ourselves, and see with a more reflective approach.

You will also be able to see how you have changed within the process, what you are grateful, how you perceive yourself, your relationships and whether your environments are right for you. To be able to recognise what serves you and what does not serve you joy and purpose, with the objective of a healthier you, Mind, Body. Heart and Soul.

By writing our desires and dreams, it again brings the emotion to the physical, the initial process of manifestation, it is closer to reality.

Take a moment or however long you need to breathe, to be in the moment, to be still, quietening the mind. I would recommend using the Grounding and Connection Guided Meditation to initiate and support this process. You may find writing starts to allow your mind to be in the present moment, becoming a download of one's thoughts.

Subscribe and access Grounding & Connecting Meditation
https://www.theinfinityhealthhub.com/free-meditation

There is no right or wrong, there are no judgements, simply allow one's heart to open and spill your mind, thoughts and emotions.

Listen to one's true heart desires, to release and liberate oneself from those restrictive thought patterns such as "I have, I need, I should do."

When one feels and recognises these restrictive thought patterns coming to the surface, which layer behind each of our thoughts and actions in our journey, ask the innocent question WHY? To unpeel and follow these thought patterns and layers, to get to the root, you may need to ask WHY several times.

You may feel yourself avoiding these questions, possibly feeling uneasy, unsure as to what may be unearthed, which is normal. You may consciously know what you need to see, however, do not wish to, as once it is acknowledged, it may bring about change, which brings uncertainty, rocking one's perception of "security" and "safety" in life. Simply by acknowledging these resistant thoughts and emotions, is the start of the process, try not to expect too much of yourself, maintain this kind, supportive and loving space for yourself.

To follow our heart desires, one's needs to feel supported, secure and to trust that one will be held throughout this evolutionary process, thus challenging all of us to release our illusionary perception of control in life, a false sense of feeling safe and secure.

Allow yourself to let your mind-heart and pen to paper flow. Hold space to allow the raw truth, emotions and heart desires to form in ink. Without being honest with yourself, you cannot move forward in life, and the same patterns resurface themselves until they are wholly acknowledged and embraced.

The key also is to remember to be loving and kind to oneself when looking within, this isn't an excuse to make yourself feel unworthy or not enough. This is simply an honest reflection of your life as a whole, to enable you to grow and transform and evolve to one's heart desires.

Ultimately in life, is it not simply to hold love, joy, peace, gratitude, fulfillment and contentment within our mind, body and core? When reviewing each aspect of one's life, ask how highly these emotions lay within, and whether one's heart desires more, and why so?

Self-Reflection Exercise

Health and Wellbeing

Our mind and body have an intrinsic and inseparable relationship. Our emotions, thoughts; traumas, if not released, become reflected within our bodies often developing into niggles, pain, discomfort, illness and dis-ease, forming a tapestry to be recognised, understood to be reflected and acted upon.

On a scale of 1-10, where do you place you, your wellbeing and health in terms of importance on this scale?

(1) You feel that you in comparison to others, are not important and unworthy and you put the wellbeing of others before yours.

(10) You hold love and kindness for yourself and understand that your health and wellbeing is imperative, and it is within your control to influence your health, working on a daily basis to maintain a healthy lifestyle

I invite you to write here in this book or a journal — date it, so you can come back and reflect once again and see how much you have grown.

Relationships Love and Compassion –

It is our relationship with ourselves, that determines our external relationships; be they family, friends, colleagues and neighbours. Therefore, if you desire to attract from others more love and kindness into your life, to be held in more respect, to be recognised for your worth, the first relationship that you need to look within, is with this beautiful person… You!

On a scale 1-10 how much kindness and self-love do your hold for yourself?

(1) You believe you are undeserving of love; you constantly criticise and judge yourself, your looks, your body, and your abilities. You find yourself in a negative downward spiral of self-loathing or dislike. You constantly seek and need love and acceptance from others, by giving so much of yourself and do not feel it is often appreciated or returned. Praise and a nice comment from another person raises your spirits making your day, yet the slightest negatively perceived comment from another can bring you tumbling down.

(10) You hold unconditional love and light in your heart for yourself. Believing in the rules of attraction, the more love and compassion you hold in your heart which overflows to others, the more it attracts. You hold kindness, self-acceptance of your abilities knowing that "You are enough, just the way you are".

Socially many of us follow an old restrictive thought pattern believing that loving oneself is arrogant and to be "full of oneself". Our life experiences from childhood to present day, influence this perception and sadly through traumas and abuse; one may have been conditioned to believe one is not worthy of love, often feeling guilty if you put your needs before others.

When we act through love and compassion, we act upon the higher resonance and highest good. This higher vibration improves our health and wellbeing, holding love and joy in our hearts; we become a vulnerable yet courageous and strong force in life that supports us and others.

Again, I invite you to write here in this book or a journal – date it, so you can come back and reflect once again and see how much you have grown.

Notice- that you may find one day you are high *"vibing"* as a 10, and the next right down to a 1 – like a DJ with their mixing set, scratching the two records to transition to the next-

This is Transformation, this is called growth – as we grow we meet our barriers of fear, quite often with a hefty serving of self-doubt and imposter phenomenon.

So when this does show up for you, know that you are on a next level of transformation and expansion – be compassionate and aware of such – and do not let the negative thoughts gain traction – call them out – thank that rogue on your shoulder, AKA ego for showing light on your fears and your illusions that block you from you truth, that is love, joy and peace!

Fear is really Courage Being Known

And that Tears are Joy Finally Coming Home

Lyrics from "She Moves Me" - Savanna

LOVE2Heal

7.

OUR EXTERNAL EXPERIENCES MIRRORS OUR INTERNAL WORLD–
The Importance of self-reflection and self-love
Written on 12-02-2021 (1202-2021) Walking the talk!

Our external world mirrors our internal world. The challenges and relationships that we find ourselves in reflects our internal thoughts and emotions, the level of self-love, unconditional love, kindness and self-acceptance we hold for ourselves within our hearts.

Throughout my life it has been a level of self-attack, mind overpowering my heart, self-love has never until recently, been something that came "naturally" to me, it was always something I rejected or felt repulsed by, my thoughts were I was undeserving to receive, I have carried a heavy voice of inner criticism and self-judgement.

In my mid-teens I was bulimic, something that I have until now, felt ashamed of being and have voiced only to a select few, hence this act of opening one's heart to an unknown audience through this writing, I place myself in a perceived vulnerable state, yet in a space of self-love and acceptance.

Normally it would have raised a huge wave of stone cold fear within me, within my gut, my stomach, bringing panic and the fear of not being good enough, the fear of being rejected. Which now writing, seeing this in black and white, it occurs to me that making myself sick was an act to release this burden, the heaviness of fear residing in my stomach, my solar plexus, where suppressed fears of emotion are stored.

Yet throughout this last year or more, I have walked within a path of trust, a path of surrendering to only love and light. This path of trust has highlighted, brought to the surface my deep rooted fears that no longer serve me, and gradually, step by step I have become more liberated, by teasing free of the grips of fear that has suffocated and restricted me in my life.

Upon opening of my heart in a state of trust, I open myself to receive more love, and the first person I need to love and hold love for, is me, creating a self-loving environment around me to support and heal.

Opening one's heart is like tapping into and creating a stronger connection to the internal power, strength and energy of my heart, thus creating more opportunities, more love and joy in my life, more self-acceptance and peace within.

For when we trust to open our hearts, to allow oneself to be "vulnerable" we are being held by the energy and frequency of our hearts, we are tapping into this immense strength and power already within us, it becomes our anchor of support.

Metaphysics has proven, that Energy attracts Energy, hence when we connect and open to the frequency the energetic waves of love and joy, we only receive the same frequency in return, amplifying through the law of constructive wave interference. We gradually become our own beacon of light and love, transmitting and receiving the expansive frequency of love and joy in its entirety.

As a baby, we are born with this light and love in us, it is what created us. Within a month or so of a new-born baby's life, once they know their basic needs will be attended to, the first interaction with their carer and guardian is a smile, a smile that becomes this beautiful deep connection that quite simply melts ones heart, a connection and exchange of unconditional love.

This expanding, infinite love becomes more constricted and reserved depending on one's life's experiences; the environment which we are exposed to when growing up throughout our foundation years, from conception to early twenties; how the patterns from our guardians/parents are imprinted within us; the moulding into restrictive socially "acceptable" behaviours and old belief systems, fuelled by the primitive fear of rejection or not being good enough.

These experiences triggers the formation of walls within our hearts, for the fear of rejection and hurt, our deep rooted base survival instincts, constricting and dimming this joyous expanding energy that is naturally within us, closing the opportunities of how much love and joy we receive.

We are a transmitter, a beacon of our internal thoughts and thus the external world reflects this back to us to see. However, this reflection within events and relationships are often seen as confirmation of our thoughts, becoming a self-perpetuating cycle of these thought patterns and being.

Therefore, for us to grow and create, to expand our lives of opportunities, abundance, love, joy and happiness, we need to allow time and space to reflect within, to understand what frequency we are transmitting into the world. To create a self-loving, kind non-judgemental supportive space, that provides a foundation to understand what no longer serves us joy, and restricts us from being our true potential, our brightest light.

To seek objectively with transparency, to shine the light upon one's self-created obstacles, fears, thoughts, emotions and belief systems that have become ingrained within us, through our life's experiences and traumas stored on a physical cellular level, which become a state of contraction, diminishing our joy.

I have such creative ideas and visions, which light me up. However, at times a sudden stone laden fear lands heavily in my gut, shaking and unnerving me, telling me that it is not possible, that it is too scary, too hard, it/I will not be good enough, which is encouraging me to shrink back within, as it is saying "it's safer here…it's safer in this shadow of fear", at least I know what will happen, right?

However, nothing necessarily positive will happen if I remain in this restrictive state of fear, it would be a self-perpetuating cycle of events, upon which my growth is limited.

"Fears are not worth what you are missing out of!"

Upon recognition of this internal critique and voice, I have the choice to decide whether to tune into the frequency of love, to choose love instead, to forge a coherence of heart and mind. Through raw and honest self-reflection in the space of self-love and self-acceptance, I am liberated from the chains of restrictions and become the co-creator of my life, my journey.

Take time to tune in, to self-reflect and to connect with one's heart, the inner anchor and strength of our being.

Affirmations-

"I release all that serves me no joy"

"My heart is open to the frequency of love and joy in its entirety"

"I walk upon a path of trust, guided by the light of love and joy"

"My heart is open to give and receive unconditional love"

"Everything I need is Already within me"

"My Heart is my Anchor, my Love is my Strength"

Daily self-care:

Creating a Loving Space, Connection & Reflection

Our external world, relationships and environment is a reflection of our internal world of thoughts and emotions and our relationship with ourselves.

Seek time every day to create a kind, loving non-judgemental space for yourself, your thoughts and emotions.

Within this space of self-acceptance, self-care and self-love, seek for what doesn't serve you joy or love.

Set the intention to release these un-serving thoughts, beliefs, fears and emotions and hold space and connection to your heart.

Connect to your heart with your hands placed on your chest, right hand over your left and feel your warmth, love, the rhythm of your heart beat, and the flow of your breath.

Feel the comfort and reassurance of these sensations, open your heart to receive and embrace more love. Feel this strength and support that is already within you.

Allow a smile to form to increase the flow of love and joy into your heart, and know that you have got this!

Open Our Hearts

I invite you to journal any thoughts and self-reflections and any other affirmations that resonate with you personally

8.

OUR BODY'S TAPESTRY– WHAT IS YOUR BODY TRYING TO TELL YOU?

...Our bodies are intricate layers of the physical and emotional...

... As we listen to our bodies and unpeel each layer of ourselves we find the cause...

...Through this ENLIGHTENMENT we have EMPOWERMENT...

Many of my clients will come to me because they are in physical pain. For me to be able to help my clients to find health and wellbeing mind and body, I need to understand WHY they are in pain, what the primary cause is, and to follow the trail and pattern of restrictions within their body.

The disciplines that I trained in are Sports and Remedial Massage, Myofascial Release, Visceral Manipulation and Reiki. When I started working with the fascia, this was *my eureka* moment! It was the form and level of connection, to merge these disciplines to enable a 3D, 4D and 5D approach to our mind, body, heart and soul.

Fascia has been described as a three-dimensional body stocking or web, enveloping each and every structure of the body, each having its own fascia sheath. The primitive cells within the embryo stage of our development form this fascia sheath from our central nervous system, encompassing the nerves, arteries, soft tissues, muscles, ligaments and tendons, the skeletal system to our skin, the outer sheath enveloping our bodies as one.

If there were a magical substance that could dissolve all parts of the body except the fascia, a complete representation would remain of the body, down to the expression of our face.

In a normal, healthy and hydrated state, the fascia has the ability to move without restriction. However, due to our general lifestyles, having postural imbalances, accidents, emotional trauma or repetitive strain injuries, it is common for the fascia to develop restrictions. Therefore, as fascia is entirely continuous throughout the body, a tear or scarring of the tissue will affect other parts within the body.

With quiet listening hands, connecting and following the fascia web of the body, it draws me into the adhesion(s) to its point-of-ease, and by continuing this direction and holding the body, it allows my hands to connect deeper. Through further listening to the body it communicates whether the restriction needs to be elongated and opened by movement away from its point-of ease, or to remain held within its fulcrum of comfort.

Following and listening to the dance of the tissues the adhesion softens and releases, often feeling like the body has melted giving a sigh of relief. The client may experience this release through; taking a deep breath; feeling the pain and discomfort release and dissolve away; feel a wave of warmth or heat rise through their body and they may also feel emotional as the body holds and stores unresolved emotions.

An intrinsic part of this physical and emotional healing is for the client to be able to slow down from their lives, and to find time to truly listen to their body. Chronic pain and injuries are generally a development of adhesions and restrictions, forming a compensatory response overtime, which eventually can no longer be held - something gives way.

The tapestry of our lives are represented within our bodies, the unresolved physical and emotional traumas, child birth, accidents, surgery, medication and the general day-to-day life. Our perceived requirements and stresses are all held within our bodies, creating physical adhesions and restrictions. The body will often highlight this through "niggly" or minor health issues, the body is waving a little white flag for us to listen to and to take notice, and the required actions.

However, we do not always listen to these issues, the white flag. We most likely see these as the body being "a pain", as it is not letting us do what we want to do at the pace we wish to do it at! We may get annoyed with our bodies, as it is perceived as a sign of getting old, or you feel the only option is to take medication, which most likely masks the symptoms rather than address the cause.

So rather than listening to our bodies to truly understand what love and care it needs, we ignore them and continue on our ways. Our bodies then become more fatigued, forming more adhesions and restrictions, possibly impacting the functionality of the organs, until the body is unable to continue in this way. As a way for our bodies to protect itself, it increases the symptoms so that they cannot be ignored. It waves a large red flag, such as acute pain that we can barely move, disease or an illness.

It is at this point we take notice and seek medical help and hopefully a professional therapist like myself, hoping you will be fixed and back on your way, back to normal, similar to your car or bike.

However, our beautiful and intelligent bodies are not just a vehicle that does what our minds want to do, they are a part of us, and they need to be listened to, honoured and loved by us. To heal we have to look within ourselves with honesty and vulnerability, maybe there are painful memories or patterns in one's life that are being held by the body, and to be truly free, these emotions need to be acknowledged, accepted and released.

By bringing attention to our bodies, to listen and connect by touch, breath and meditation we gain knowledge and realisation, it empowers us to be able to unpeel these layers to heal our bodies and our mind.

9.

HEALING THROUGH THE E-MOTION OF LOVE

Listen-Observe-Visualise-Empower

Insanity is doing the same thing over and over again and expecting a different result.

Albert Einstein

Let me share an example of one of my clients, it may on a certain level, resonate with you too.

A client comes to me presenting chronic back pain, which they have suffered with for several years; they are debilitated with the pain and are considering surgery. Following a comprehensive consultation I start to see a picture and pattern unfolding about their body.

Imagine a person who had a trauma earlier in their life, this experience made them wary of the future, they felt out of control, they felt stressed and worried as they were still holding onto this trauma, mostly likely rooted within their subconscious.

To rationalise and control these fears, fear of the unknown, fear of rejection and in the attempt to feel at "ease" with life, they begin to plan and control every aspect of their life, possibly other people within their lives, believing that no other unexpected traumas would happen again, because they have it "under control".

Unbeknown to them, this way of being becomes the norm to them; it becomes a part of their character and way of life.

Through this worry, stress and tension and holding onto the trauma, the intestines and digestion system becomes restricted and irritated. Physically this restricts the activation of the parasympathetic vagus nerve, due to the heightened state of the fight/flight sympathetic nervous system, which overtime causes an inflammatory response within the digestive system. They start to experience symptoms of indigestion and feeling bloated with the odd lower back pain and twinge. To subdue these symptoms they take medication and continue their ways.

The adhesions become greater and more restricted within the intestines, they start to find they cannot tolerate as many foods anymore. They feel more fatigued than normal, more bloated with a fluctuation of bowel movements, generally feel more stressed and anxious, experience mood swings and tend to overreact to situations more. The back, becomes more restricted with increased pain, they cannot do as much, this is put down to just getting older, so it is simply accepted as this, so they take medication to subdue the symptoms and carry on their life in a restricted way.

The adhesions and restrictions increase within the digestion system, they start getting sharp pain in their groin and hip area, often referring down their leg. Their back stops them from doing the activities that they enjoy, they feel so much more inhibited in their movements and feel more fatigued and debilitated from this discomfort.

They seek medical help and increase their medication to reduce the pain, practicing a few stretches yet with no resolution.

Becoming quite frustrated and angry with themselves and their body as they cannot stop nor control it, not knowing what else to do, feeling lost, down, depressed, which brings in further anxiety. The situation is challenging them how they have always conducted themselves, being in control. They are considering surgery as this seems like their only option available, what else could they do?

As a last resort, they seek "alternative" help, they find me.

Through the detailed consultation, I see a correlation of the digestive symptoms of fatigue, food intolerances, indigestion and the back pain. Listening to the body I am directed to the lower left hip towards the groin, this is where the sigmoid colon is located. The colon nerve supply is through the lower back, it is also linked by fascia to the femoral nerve and artery which supplies the hip and leg. I am also drawn to the small intestines which has an indirect attachment to the spine through its blood and nerve supply the Mesentery root. Restrictions here will cause pain in the lower back, also having a ripple effect of the whole musculoskeletal system.

Emotionally, the intestines are affected by over-worry and anxiousness, a tendency to be over-protective of one's family. These emotions cause tensions within the gut, you may have heard of "tying oneself up in knots", hence the functionality of the intestines are reduce in absorbing key nutrients, which are vital for our overall health, our energy levels and immune system, paving way to food intolerances, lowered immune system and fatigue.

Energetically, the underlying fears, the fears of survival are held in our base chakra, which is our foundation, where we question, am I safe, am I supported? If blocked emotionally/energetically, our feet to our lower back and our adrenal glands are affected, as this is one of the first parts of the body that would need to be activated when in the fight/flight response.

Through explanation of the connection, whereas the client before had thought all of the symptoms were unrelated, they are enlightened and empowered to be able to make positive changes within their life to help themselves heal.

Alongside the physical treatments, connecting and releasing the trauma held within the body, they practise diaphragmatic breathing and meditation, to activate the vagus nerve and improve vagal tone, which is imperative for our health and wellbeing.

The breathing and meditation finds and holds space within the mind and body, to release un-serving restrictive thoughts patterns and emotions. They follow a healthy balanced gut-healing diet and hydration, to improve the function of the digestive and immune system, to cleanse the body of toxins physical and emotional. They practice restorative exercise such as yoga to release adhesions within the fascia, the connective web.

Their pain gradually reduces, they feel much more positive and relaxed about life, things do not stress them out like they used to, they are calm and at peace within their body.

This is a beautiful example as to how our physical, emotion and energetic bodies are all part of the one, us! Therefore to truly heal, we need to look at ourselves in a 3D, 4D, even 5D level, as our bodies are a representation of all and becomes an awakening/ a call to action when we experience pain and dis-ease.

Thus, when we experience pain, restrictions, dis-ease, we need to slow down and understand what our body is seeking, how is it asking us to change and to hold a loving space upon which the mind and body can heal. So in an odd way, we need to love pain!

We begin to learn the language of our body and our Soul in some way, as this innate wisdom seeks reconnection, coherence and alignment.

10.

WHAT IS SELF-LOVE?

"Holding unconditional love for ourselves, is a challenge we should all aspire to!"

Self-love for me, is holding unconditional love and kindness in your heart for you, allowing yourself to let go of your inner fears and criticisms through awareness of self-reflection and self-acceptance. It is about holding a space for your thoughts that is kind and supportive with no judgement.

It is coming to the understanding that you are enough, just the way you are, you do not have to be anything else, you do not need to prove yourself to others and especially not to yourself. As ultimately to achieve pure unconditional love for oneself with no ego, is a lifetime's achievement I believe for many of us.

Through connection to this inner power and strength of love within our hearts, we are connecting to an expansive energy that reaches beyond what our minds can compute. The universal frequency of love supports the progression of joy, to peace and enlightenment. Surely if but all we achieve in this lifetime is this inner joy, happiness and peace, this is an achievement in itself?

Seeking happiness through the conditioned external material world, an old belief system and accepted story, portrayed to provide happiness, is a mirage, the act of chasing for the gold under the rainbow.

This mirage of contentment and happiness, is always just out of reach, as it is not something that can be found outside of oneself, it is the internal love and connection to what is already within, that will provide love, purpose, contentment, joy and peace.

Imagine the liberation from understanding that what we need is already within us, within our core and our hearts; it is a matter of attaining the key of self-love to open and tap into this resource.

This external race to the end of the rainbow causes a tsunami of suppressed stress in mind and body. Caught in the past, possible traumas and limited beliefs that have become imprinted in you, and fear of the unknown, very rarely being in the still of the present moment. Not allowing our body to rest and heal within the parasympathetic nervous state, thus having a detrimental effect on our health and wellbeing over a prolonged period of time.

Striving hard to reach and gain, to only hold a hollow victory even if one's goals are gained externally, continuing the search for the next thing, the next "achievement", to prove that you are good enough or to feel contented! Attaining in life these material things of cars, houses, high profile jobs, lots of followers on social media for instance, are all achievements, however, when they become a necessity to prove you are good enough, it has the similar outcome to a Roman Chariot race.

However, this strive externally may often reaffirm these inner feelings of inadequacy, which is common for all when we seek happiness or the need to have confirmation that we a good enough in the absence of self-love. It is part of our genetic primitive makeup, to hold fears of not being good enough, the fear of rejection, the fear of the unknown.

For a few moments, place your hands on your heart, feel the rhythm and strength of your heart beat, feel the steady reassurance and comfort of the flow of your breath, focus and tune into these sensations; permit oneself to open one's heart, to know that it is safe to do so.

How does your chest feel, do you feel an opening, a magnetism; a sense of strength and power that feels it could hold and lift you, if you trusted and surrendered to this expansive energy, this deep connection to one's heart of pure love and light for oneself?

You may hopefully find a moment of stillness, of calm and inner peace, a liberation and freedom of one's inner voice, releasing thoughts, doubts, judgement and criticisms, the voice of our ego.

This ego, isn't the classic ego of a derogative way to describe someone who appears full of themselves, an external judgement. Yes they have an ego, however, probably not in the way one has perceived them to be, it is probably their ego of self-doubt that is pushing them to exert this self-defending image.

We are tribal beings that need one another, the joy, comfort and reassurance of touch of one another, the simple act of a hug, something that we have all been very made aware of since 2020, due to the restrictions of physical connection.

However, we do not need our tribes today in the same way. We needed our tribes/communities for our basic survival, to be protected, to be safe, to be provided for. Therefore, if we were rejected and outcast from our tribe through either not being good enough, weak, of not speaking the same story of the tribe, our chances of survival were pretty limited on our own.

Our basic needs are generally met now, a roof over our heads, clean running water and food on our tables, hence our evolved domestication has different requirements from our tribal connection. However, it is understandable that in our current times these genetic, primal, deep rooted fears still play a part in our life, migrating and acting towards the perceived socially acceptable behaviour to avoid rejection.

For instance, showing an open heart of emotion expressing one's vulnerabilities, resurrects a fear of showing a weakness with the potential of rejection. Our ego tells us a story that our peers may question this honesty and push away. Although, it most likely will be triggering their ego, to witness this honesty; probing them to look within, to question is this genuine, can it be trusted, repeating a story in their psyche.

Our ego may suggest that others may wish to take advantage of this perceived weakness, to judge and criticise, our fear of hurt. These events may be reflected if this is the internal conversation one is happening with oneself.

However, when opening one's heart when one already holds unconditional self-love and acceptance, this raw vulnerability becomes an immense strength, an act that feels most liberating, attracting only love in return.

Interestingly, should these more fearful based thoughts play out, that a "friend" wishes to take advantage of your perceived weakness; they are simply showing themselves to you in a light for you to see, for you in turn to decide, do you wish for them to be part of your loving supportive tribe?

This is the power of self-love and self-acceptance, you are not seeking this unstable stability externally from other people, as you already have this strength within you. Instead, you receive in return the same frequency, love, as energy attracts energy. From a higher expansive perspective of love you see the raw truth with full awareness and objectivity.

Our evolution has provided this opportunity to choose who we have in our lives and the extent of these relationships. The more we evolve to open our hearts, we hold more awareness, see more beauty and transition to an emotional state towards inner peace and calm.

I see the ego as a frequency of fear, the red band you would have on the old fashioned radios, the other side of this radio is the expansive frequency of love, we have the choice of which station and frequency we wish to tune into.

Fear undoubtedly has a place in our lives, to keep us alive, to activate our fight/flight response; for example, to activate our bodies to make us slam on the brakes when in the car to avoid an accident, to know not to step too close to the edge of a cliff if not wearing a parachute.

However, it can become the frequency that we are tuned into daily in our perceptions and actions, and as fear is a contracted energy, it forms restrictions, blocks, a repetitive cycle of ones life's events. This fear places a restriction upon our growth, which is reflected and felt as self-perpetuating confirmation that one is not good enough.

It is like having the foot on the accelerator, the constant need to reassure one is enough through the constant stress and striving of life and achievements, seeking this acceptance and proof of oneself. Yet, having the other foot on the brake in the fear of not being good enough, as you can imagine, the car would soon fall apart.

Our bodies are the same, it stays within this freeze sympathetic nervous system, constantly stimulating and releasing hormones that overtime causes inflammation, fatigue and disease.

Our ego is this primal voice of survival with the deep undertones of fear, our basic need of survival that will always resonate within us, it is part of our DNA and fabric. Even as I write this with my understanding of the ego, I still wish for this to be good enough,

Therefore, it is not about separation of self, forming another negative war of mind and voices, generating further confusion and delusion. It is through awareness and integration of the ego, immersed in self-love for oneself, to decide on the amplitude of this voice to govern our life's journey; to recognise one's fears and upon self-reflection and with the act of free will, to choose love and light instead.

For it is the ego that can take credit for where you are today and what you have achieved, without conscious awareness it has been the driving force for you to learn and expand your mind.

However, the key to health and happiness, is being conscious as to what the driver is now, from this moment onwards – is it fear or is it love – are you in alignment with your Heart and Soul?

Is it a subconscious and unconscious programming from generations ingrained into our mind, body, blood and bones, our DNA – or are your thoughts, actions and intentions coming from a conscious state of being – of self-awareness?

For your conscious choice is your power and your awareness is your superpower!

Awareness Creates Conscious Choices

Hence, the importance of self-care, setting aside time and space to connect with one's heart, to allow this infinite love and light to flow within you, like a waterfall of golden light through your crown.

Owning this love in your heart for you, to know that you are loved and you are love, that you are supported and that you are enough!

Embracing and accepting that you deserve to be loved, because you are love and to allow it to flow into you entire body, until this love and light overflows from your heart for others to receive.

Even though this energy is infinite, we need to connect daily to refuel to regenerate, to find a balance of receiving and giving. Quite often we give so much, believing that we are not worthy of love and become drained and fatigued. Often demoralised as one is giving so much yet not receiving it back from others, an act of seeking externally of what already lays within.

It is our responsibility to set aside time to connect and refuel, to be self-aware and recognise when we need to do this. Hence, having a daily practice of stillness, breathing and meditation morning and night, is an act of topping ones' energy levels up, to remain grounded and connected with oneself and to avoid the vortex of stress draining our physical and mental health.

It is like brushing our teeth, the usual routine of preparing one's body for the day and evening, meditation is an act of cleansing and preparation of the mind each day.

This regular practice strengthens the connection and self-awareness; it provides more of an objective perspective to self-reflect, in a non-judgemental space of self-love and kindness, to understand whether our thoughts, emotions, perceptions and actions are of love or of fear.

This ultimately will highlight our voice of ego, if it is not of love, then it is one's ego.

11.

THE PYJAMA REVOLUTION
The Founding of the Pyjama Revolution

It was through self-love that I had the inspiration and motivation to set up the Pyjama Revolution meditation group, to share this experience and to support others on their path of self-love, self-acceptance and healing. A space for those who wish to connect their mind and body, to become more empowered to heal emotionally and physically, through the beautiful form of guided meditation.

The vision for this group was to be a supportive web and space where people know they can simply be themselves, with no judgement, just love, kindness and joy.

It came to me when I was walking my puppy early one morning whilst in my Pyjamas, crocs and socks, not reading overly high on the stylish chic level! However, I realised that I did not care how I looked, not because of lack of pride or love for myself; it was in fact the complete opposite.

From holding love in my heart for myself, it freed me from my inner criticisms and fears of the possible critique or judgement from others, it was an eureka moment!

At that very moment of realisation, I felt so much joy, love and gratitude in my heart. I felt liberated baring a huge smile on my face…probably looking like I had been let out for the day…but hey ho!

My experience through my own journey and my clients, I have witnessed many heal emotionally and physically when love and kindness for ourselves are held within our hearts.

When we connect and hold this light and love in our hearts, we begin to release our inner fears that hold us back in life, the fears of not being good enough, or the fear of being rejected, which under-layers many of us, due to our autonomic survival instinct.

Through what we have experienced in these recent times individually and globally, my belief and vision for us beings is to evolve from opening our hearts, holding love and kindness for ourselves, releasing these fears of vulnerability and then to allow love and acceptance to overflow to others.

Through this love, we hold a space, an invisible web of light that holds and supports us individually and collectively.

A space that can be reached out to whenever it is needed, to know that someone out there cares and that you are never alone.

Open Our Hearts

12.

TO BREATHE OR TO NOT TO BREATHE- THAT IS THE QUESTION?
The Healing Power of Breath

Our Breath is the Bridge from Mind to Body to Soul

It would sound very obvious to state that breathing is important, however, it is equally vital for our health and wellbeing mind and body in HOW we breathe!

I bet you are suddenly more aware of your breath right now…good!

Our breath is our connection to the universe, the field of energy that is the collective for all, the collective of individuals, the Earth and her creatures upon which all breathe and exchange the substance of life, oxygen.

The majority of my clients who are suffering with pain especially within the neck-shoulder region, headaches and migraines, stress and anxiety, insomnia, digestion issues, asthma and COPD, the list can go on, do not breathe correctly, thus causing stress and fatigue for their bodies. Simply, it is pretty much the majority of my lovely clients!

From demonstrating diaphragmatic and deep abdominal breathing and working with my clients for just five minutes during their treatment, they can feel the difference. Their bodies soften, their eyes and muscles in their face relax and their bodies start to let go, quite often experiencing an emotional release. A wave of calm washes over them-hello to the parasympathetic nervous system!

I often get funny *"you're-kinda-crazy"* looks at the beginning, when I say breath through your stomach. However, once my logic behind this "madness" is explained, it is often the *"eureka"* moment for my clients and can be most empowering for them, knowing that they can help their own health and wellbeing, through the power of their breath.

In the moment when we are born, each of us signal our independence with a breath and a sound. Our autonomic nervous system instinctively supports our breath through nerves, organs and soft tissue, to take our first inhalation representing the start of our independent life.

This is the beginning of the exchange and balance of our being on planet Earth, our inhalation of oxygen, the gas that triggered evolution and through the metabolism of our bodies we exhale carbon dioxide.

Taking one's breath is not always a conscious process that we give a huge amount of attention to, however, we know it is vital for our survival and being; we can survive days without water, weeks without food, yet only moments without oxygen.

Let's take a moment to become Conscious of our breath through this exercise

Sitting in a chair is probably the best place to be doing this exercise with your feet flat on the floor.

You might want to note down your findings, although this is not necessary. Just remember this is not a test, do not overthink it. Simply feel your breath, to initiate the connection process of your mind and body through breath.

For a moment, take several deep breaths now, you may wish to close your eyes, becoming conscious as to where you feel the inhalation breath within your body:

- Are you breathing in through your nose or mouth?
- Where do you feel your body moving?
- Is it in your upper shoulder, neck and throat area, are your shoulders rising up towards your ears, is your chest opening and your back arching backwards?
- Are these areas opening or constricting? Do you feel a tension in your throat and neck area?
- Can you feel anything move? Can you hear your breath?

- o Is your stomach and abdominal area relaxing or contracting?
- o How long are you breathing in for?

Great- Now bring your attention to your exhalation breath.
- o How long is your exhalation breath, is it the same, less or more than your in-breath?
- o Are you breathing out through your nose or mouth?
- o How does your jaw and tongue feel, are there any tensions, are you clamping your jaw down?
- o Does your body relax, collapse, does it feel supported?
- o Is it a slow and gentle or a quick inverted movement?
- o How do you feel?
- o Is there a rest for a moment between the exhalation and inhalation and the inhalation to exhalation?

Now imagine a young baby breathing on their backs, is their little tummy rising up and down, are their little shoulders coming up, does their breathing look relaxed, gentle and an easy process, or does it look like a work out in itself?

A healthy little baby's breathing will be relaxed and gentle with their beautiful round bellies rising up and expanding.

So when in our lifetime does our way of breathing change, what affects the way we breathe? This will vary for each individual through our physical, social and emotional environments and relationships from birth to now, and our physical ways of being within our mind and body.

As we become more static in prolonged postures, our bodies form restrictions and postural compensations within our physical form. Injuries and surgery, all have an impact on the optimum breath cycle, by restricting the balanced movement of the respiratory system, the surrounding musculoskeletal and visceral systems and the web of fascia that connects it all as one. Hence, movement and expansion through breath and exercise is key to our health.

From an embryo stage of development within the womb, the primitive cells, the building blocks of the fascia, at about 2 weeks form the "primitive streak". These cells then loop and fold themselves either side of the primitive streak, enclosing it and creating a groove that will become the neural canal, our central nervous system. This is the control centre for the brain and spinal cord, supporting the delicate process of communication via the network of nerves.

Incredibly, this looping and folding process of the primitive cells also becomes our skin, our outer protection and sheath, the largest sensory organ of our bodies. The cells that form the very centre of our being, also forms our most outer self, hence whatever touches the outer skin produces a response within the inner self.

Our internal and external systems are not separate they are one, exchanging stimuli and responses to each other, highlighting the healing power of touch increased through the connection to the fascia.

This wonderful intrinsic relationship becomes a sensory to our environment, it informs us if we are safe, it helps us connect and read others within this environment and atmosphere. However, small or seemingly insignificant, will stimulate a response, an impression within, which most often will affect the way in which we breathe. It is the stimulus that choreographs our first breath.

Our breath and our health are affected through our physical environment, the quality of air that we breathe, the imbalance of gases and toxicity, as a consequence to our impact collectively on the Earth and the environment. Our breath and the way one breathes adapts to this stimulus to maintain the intake of oxygen.

Our emotional environment growing up, how nurture forms us, beginning from conception, within our Mother's womb, her emotional state and being at the time. Our epigenetics, how we were born, to the cutting of the umbilical cord; how we were taught to express or to suppress our emotions, through being the observer of our guardians and from our own experiences.

A young child is able to connect to their parent's emotions through this sensory being. Our theta brain wave state, absorbs our environment to the subconscious, sensing the level of love or pain within the parent, becoming a response within our own body as a child.

When one is growing up in a healthy, safe and loving

environment, with the supportive space to express oneself emotionally to process and release, one's breath is open and expansive, our light and joy flows effortlessly with ease and grace.

However, if this foundation stage of one's growth and upbringing is not a safe environment, or a platform to express one's emotions, we begin to retract within, holding tension in the mind and body. This tightens the abdominal area and the organs within, restricting the movement of the diaphragm, the vital muscle of the respiratory system.

The questioning of one's safety, emotional nourishment and fear-based responses, heightens the stimulus of our sympathetic nervous system, unbalancing the equilibrium and health of our body and mind.

Even with the most supportive upbringing, our journey from childhood to adulthood, we are being groomed socially to be accepted into this "socially constricted" environment.

This training of acceptable behaviour initiates the emotional process to contain oneself, to suppress and mask our emotions, constricting our bodies to hold these emotions. Predominantly within the visceral organs, which all connect with the respiratory system through the web of fascia, causing adhesions and restriction. Thus the body constantly adapts to these tension patterns to ensure one can still breathe.

If you picture a toddler having an absolute "paddy" because they can't have a toy that another child has, without adult intervention after a while, they would probably take a deep breath and sniffle and go and find something else to play with, and most likely forget what had just happened, back in the moment of joy with the new found toy. They are freely expressing and releasing their emotions, they are activating the primal release within the limbic system and function of our brain.

Fast forward to this child at school, where another child takes their favourite pencil, this child has gradually been conditioned to not overly react, they most likely want to snatch their pencil back and/or hit the other child, however, they do not, as they are being programmed to retain their emotion and for the fear of the consequences. They are suppressing their emotions to an "acceptable level".

These emotions if not released, become stored within our cells in a contracted form, enclosed by the cell receptors. The cell and fascia become restricted pulling in, and overtime, drawing other cells inwards. This limits the gliding element of the fascia, causing a more inhibitive motion of the visceral organs and breath, which causes a friction against self, thus heat and inflammation – the root to pain and dis-ease!

The young child will instinctively release these emotions yet only when they feel safe and supported to do so. When that loving parent or guardian collects the child from school, they seem moody, angry, upset, overwhelmed, subconsciously working through these suppressed emotions.

Often misunderstood by the adult, it may be interpreted as the frustration is directed at them and wish to resolve and dampen the fire as quickly as possible and/ or become offended and shift emotionally away from the child, as the adult's inner child may be triggered.

However, when one understands this is a release process for the child and not a personal trigger, and the adults' role is to maintain a safe and loving space for them to move these emotions out of their system. A trip to the park after school with snacks and a hug, is probably the most nourishing way to help release and support this emotional release.

The same applies to us as adults, to support the release of these emotions; we need a safe compassionate and non-judgemental space, held in self-love and kindness, alongside physical movement.

As our breath is our relationship to our internal and external self and our environment physically, emotionally and socially, it would seem wise to start with the way we breathe, to expand our breath, our mind and our body.

Our breath is the bridge and connection of our mind and body, to our physical and emotional self and to our internal and external relationship of our environment. It is the foundation to holding equilibrium of health within mind and body as one. It is the resource, the supportive and sustainable inner tool that we can use to initiate the release of emotions that no longer serve us.

How are these tensions reflected in our body and posture?

As the body contracts inwardly to protect itself emotional and physically through the sheath of fascia, the abdominal area housing our digest organs, restricts and tightens! This inhibits the diaphragm to perform its key movement, to lower within the abdomen and glide over the abdominal organs, to expand the thoracic area to inhale. These tensions form an imbalance of pressure internally, and its relationship to the external environment.

Rather than a relaxed effortlessly flowing breath, of the diaphragm freely contracting and moving, with the abdominal area moving inferiorly and forwards (belly out and down), our breath becomes more laboured, and requires other fascia sheaths and muscles to work harder, to inhale and expand the rib cage.

As the diaphragm completes approximately 22,000 movements per day (8 million+ per year), pulling and pushing our lungs and abdominal viscera along with it each time, we can start to understand how and why physical restrictions and postural changes form. When our breath cycle isn't working to its optimum movement, it causes fatigue and secondary adhesions through compensation and pain.

The body is amazing and will adapt to its new environment internally and externally to maintain life and movement, however these compensative responses, forms imbalance, thus further postural adjustments, restrictions and adhesions.

The adhesions form a "Hansel and Gretel" trail through the fascia web, upon which, when followed guides one through a path and sequence of adhesions, unearthing layers of the physical and the emotional.

When the diaphragm is unable to follow its optimum movement, the accessory respiratory muscles are activated via a neural pathway, becoming more of the prime movers for inhalation; they take on more of the burden and responsibility as such, increasing the neural pathways excitability to these muscles away from the diaphragm.

The key accessory respiratory muscles are the
Sternocleidomastoid; the Pectoralis Minor; the Serratus Anterior

and the Scalenes.

Overtime, from overuse of these muscles, they become hypertonic and cause postural and fascia changes; the shoulders become protracted/come forward and inwards; the neck is drawn downwards and forwards, giving us an eye-line towards the floor. As humans, we need to see the horizon, so the muscles at the occipital area/back of the head and neck, need to remain contracted to uphold this new position, and to lift our eye line.

The area shortens and compresses the nerves and cervical vertebrae causing pain and restriction, impinging on the blood flow to the Central Nervous System (CNS), often resulting in common symptoms such as headaches and migraines.

This chronic postural position holds us in a more stressed fight/flight physical state, even if one does not feel stressed. The stress has become a new benchmark, an unsustainable platform to perform our functions long term. It is often not until we feel less stressed, that we realise that we were stressed before! This nervous state holds us more in the Sympathetic Nervous System (SNS), which I call the AMBER-alert mode, similar to leaving the car lights on, affecting our energy levels and our mental wellbeing.

The key nerve to be activated to transition into the healing, rest digest, feed and breed state, the Parasympathetic Nervous System is the Vagus Cranial Nerve X.

Part of this long and extensive nerve is located parallel and behind to the sternocleidomastoid muscle, within the carotid fascia sheath, housing and protecting the carotid artery and the internal jugular vein.

The vagus nerve's relationship with these affect their functions, hence if not activated through being constricted, such as tight muscles and fascia, it causes a dysfunction of the vein and arterial function, affecting the drainage of the skull, brain, superficial face and most of the neck and the blood supply to the head and neck.

This position of tension results in symptoms such as, high blood pressure, headaches, migraines, oedema, and tension with the neck, head and shoulders.

This wonderful nerve is intrinsic to our health and equilibrium and deserves a book in itself. This nerve also passes through the hiatus of the diaphragm alongside the abdominal aorta and oesophagus. Any restrictions in the diaphragm would restrict the function and activation of all these.

Generating a variety of symptoms such as, indigestion, inflammation, IBS, stomach reflux, reduced circulation in the lower limbs. and overtime because of the vagus nerves impact on the health of the digestion and immune system, food intolerances, autoimmune diseases, depression, anxiety, mineral absorption, chronic fatigue, fibromyalgia, arthritis and anything else with 'itis' (inflammation).

These examples are highlighting that how we breathe determines our level of health and wellbeing, and how intrinsically linked our breath, our emotions and our physical body are.

Forming a mindfulness of your breath and how you breathe becomes a key to unlocking and empowering your own health.

13.

HOMEOSTASIS BY BREATH

When we look upon our bodies with admiration and love- we can truly hold space for our mind and body as one - to become a foundation of self-care and empowerment.

It is often perceived that our bodies are a machine, a machine to carry out the will of our minds, which causes frustration and detachment when it begins to malfunction. However, our bodies are not a machine, they are not separate to our minds, they are a reflection and stimuli of our internal and external environment, and our thoughts and emotions.

The body's innate wisdom has this amazing ability to adjust and manage the trillion of individual cells, to function and to return to a state of balance and homeostasis. If our body was a machine, the simplest of imbalance, such as a cog not turning correctly would cause complete malfunction.

Our bodies are an energetic force which uses energy on a massive scale via the metabolic processes. Every cell is involved in this process of breaking down energy, transporting and absorbing this energy to function. This breakdown and building up of energy requires carbohydrates, minerals, oxygen and the microbiome within the digestive system, also known as the Gut Brain, producing water, waste and CO_2. This highlights the relationship and balance of the respiratory and renal systems, the lungs and kidneys.

Our breath will adjust according to how much energy we need for the body to function, hence when running, our breathing increases to support the increased demand of oxygen, compared to if we were sitting working, watching television; our breathing slows down once the exercise has stopped or decreased in intensity.

Carbon dioxide is mostly seen as a waste gas and that it is completely expelled from our bodies when we exhale, however, maintaining a balance of CO_2 and oxygen within our cells are fundamental to the homeostasis of the body's pH levels.

Life on Earth depends on appropriate pH levels in and around living organisms and cells. Human life requires a tightly controlled pH level in the serum of about 7.4 (a slightly alkaline range of 7.35 to 7.45) to survive.

CO_2 regulates the acidity levels within the blood, hence low levels of CO_2 through more hyperventilation (breathing in more oxygen then exhaling CO_2), causes the body to move towards a higher alkaline pH, which is called respiratory alkalosis.

The high alkaline pH causes the cells to contract, restricting the blood flow, causing panic attacks. Hence when someone is experiencing a panic attack, the breathing into a paper bag is a way to quickly increase the CO_2 levels with the body, to bring back balance of the pH within the blood.

On the contrary, too much CO_2 in our blood, through the inability of excreting from our lungs and/or kidneys, increases the acidity of the body, which may lead to metabolic acidosis, when chronic.

Other symptoms of this imbalance are muscle cramps, headaches/migraines, chronic fatigue, premenstrual syndrome, cold hands and feet even in warm days, palpitations, impaired concentration, disturbed sleep patterns, heartburn, flatulence, asthma and many more. All are signs "white flags" that the body is working hard to return to homeostasis, a flag to listen to and observe, to bring about change of lifestyle of what is not serving our healthy balance.

Quite often these flags are not in isolation, which are perceived to be separate to one another, yet they are a connection, a trail of imbalance and dysfunction, and when followed through the fascia web of interconnectedness, it leads us to the cause and the required actions of self-care.

The awareness, listening and observations of our body, enables us to see these signs, which supports the fundamental process of prevention is better than cure!

If we take the example of pre-menstrual syndrome, 7-10 days prior to menstruation, the woman's progesterone hormonal levels peak. Progesterone absorbs CO_2, thus reduces the level and pH of the blood, combine this with poor breathing habits, hyperventilation, anxiousness and stress, poor nutrient absorption, all result in muscle cramps, pain, loss of concentration and brain fog, the common symptoms of PMT.

Overtime this imbalance of CO_2, visceral, nerve and arterial restrictions may affect the production of progesterone and oestrogen balance, causing an increase of the symptoms and fluctuations when women reach the transition period of menopause, an escalation of these dysfunctions, "white flags".

In summary, our breath is the key to our quality of health and life. It is the intrinsic bridge of mind and body, our internal and external self as one, it senses and adapts to environments we are within emotionally and physically.

Our breath is an inner resource providing comfort and reassurance when consciously connected with, to ground and to hold a space of internal awareness, for one's thoughts and emotions.

The rhythmically conscious flow of the breath becomes a beautifully controlled release of the subconscious emotions and unconscious patterns, which no longer serves the mind and body. Releasing toxins, promoting healing on a cellular level feeding the vital source of oxygen for optimum cell metabolism, the homeostasis and balance of our mind and body, providing a foundation of regeneration of neural and fascia pathways, to the physical sensory experience.

Breathe in and expand the joy of life to every cell and fibre of your being, exhale and release what no longer serves this joy to hold balance, connection, peace and health.

"I release all that no longer serves my joy or purpose, with the greatest comfort, ease and grace"

The Diaphragmatic Breathing Technique

Lie on your back on a flat surface or in bed, with your knees bent and your head supported. You can use a pillow under your knees to support your legs.

Place your left hand on your upper chest and heart area, and the right hand around your naval and abdominal area. This will allow you to feel your diaphragm move as you breathe.

Breathe in slowly through your nose so that your stomach moves out against your hand. Imagine a silver thread on your naval lifting your abdominal area and stomach expanding, relaxing your hips and glutes (buttock muscles) and your pelvic floor muscles (the ones we tighten to stop ourselves from peeing and pooing!)

Your left hand on your chest should remain reasonably still, concentrate on your connection with your right hand on your stomach area, breathe into your hand and naval.

As you exhale through your mouth with pursed lips, tighten your stomach and pelvic floor muscles, bringing them inward and upward (pelvic floor), as if you are trying to stop yourself going to the toilet, bringing your navel deeper to the spine. You may feel an upwards and anterior tilt of your hips

Then relax all of your muscles, let everything go, soften into what you are laying upon, this happens between the space of the exhale to inhale.

Repeat this cycle of breath, concentrating on the expansion of your lower abdominal area and the connection with your right hand as inhaling, opening the midline of the body, forming space between your hands.

On the exhale feel the flowing contraction of your body, the right hand may feel it is coming in and up towards the left hand.

It may feel rather peculiar at first, take it easy on yourself. If you find your chest wanting to expand and move, keep bringing your attention to your right hand on your stomach, focus on this connection, gradually allowing this to be the greater movement.

You may find it easier to tense the muscles that you wish to relax first. Exhale and tense the muscles, then inhale relaxing them, whichever works for you.

You may notice an increased effort will be needed to use the diaphragm correctly. At first, you'll probably get tired while doing this exercise. But keep at it, because with continued practice, diaphragmatic breathing will become easy and automatic.

Once you become familiar with these movements, see if you can take each inhale and exhale a little further. Imagine a lift and you take it up or down one more level, allowing more oxygen into your lungs and the removal of waste products.

When you first learn the diaphragmatic breathing technique, it may be easier for you to follow the instructions lying down, as you gain more practice, you can try the diaphragmatic breathing technique while sitting in a chair. To perform this exercise while sitting in a chair, ensure you are sitting comfortably, with your knees bent and your shoulders, head and neck relaxed and continue to breathe as per above.

Be conscious that you may feel dizzy during and afterwards, possibly quite spaced, so take your time in getting back to your feet, give them a tap on the ground to feel that connection and support.

Becoming emotional is normal too as you are beginning to hold space on a cellular level. The cells release these held hormones/chemicals (energetic imprints) stimulated from the emotions that have become stored within this contracted and suppressed state.

Your body will only release what you can process at this time when you hold a safe, kind and caring space for yourself. See this release as a positive stage of the healing process.

Go with the flow of your breath, should you feel emotions passing through, feel your connection with the ground of which you lay or sit upon. As you inhale, you acknowledge and accept the emotions, within the abdominal area, then without judgement or analysis, breathe out letting them go, visualise the emotions being released from your body from you heart, throat and mouth.

Continue and focus of your breath, feel its comfort and reassurance, flowing in love as one breathes in and releasing old thoughts and emotions as you breathe out.

You may wish to hold these affirmations of thoughts, *I am Safe, I am Supported, I am Loved,* as you breath in, bringing the emotion to the surface of the wave, the rising of the belly, coming to the heart plexus, where your left hand is on your body.

Then exhale, contracting, expelling and clearing the wave of emotion from the stomach- heart –throat –neck and mouth. You may wish to say to oneself *"I am releasing all that serves me no purpose, in ease and grace"*, or simply flow with the strength of the breath, carrying you through the process.

Gradually the emotions will subside, you may feel serenely still and peaceful, the calm after the storm as such. You may have an array of sensations; tired, or the reverse, energised; feel shivers and cold all of a sudden; heat; joyful; tingling within areas of the whole of the body; yawning; burping. All of these sensations are the body transitioning from the fight/flight nervous system to the parasympathetic, the state of healing.

You will not always have these emotional releases, the body is unwinding and unpeeling the layers one at a time and what is right for you at that moment. Trust that your body knows instinctively how to heal itself, it is our mind held in trauma and stress that blocks the process; allow your breath to be the inner strength, the anchor and the flow of release.

However you feel, hold space for yourself to become more grounded, come back to a gentle and easy flow of your breath, feel your feet on the ground. Start to move to work it through your system, if you can step outside and feel the earth bare foot this would be most beneficial, if too muddy and cold, hug a tree.

As we ground to the negative charged energy of the Earth, our bodies release any excess energy "static", which creates stress and dis-coherence within our body. The act of "Earthing" enables electrons to enter the body, to find a neutral balanced state. Studies have shown how our blood cells reduce clotting when grounding, and our HRV (Heart Rate Variability) improves.

If unable to do these grounding actions, grab a chunk of dark chocolate, with a high percentage of cacao, and hold it in your mouth until it dissolves- every cloud has a silver lining!! Dark chocolate is high in anti-oxidants and magnesium, which are required to support the detox function of our bodies; it also releases endorphins, the feel good hormone. It's a win-win in my eyes!

Drink plenty of water, to ground to hydrate and to aid the metabolic functions and detoxing. Do not substitute water for other drinks, unfortunately they don't count. Imagine washing and cleansing your laundry in anything but water, the clothes would not come out overly clean, most likely dirtier; the same applies to our bodies!

Setting a daily practice of diaphragmatic breathing for five to ten minutes, 3-4 times every day is a wonderful foundation for your health. You can extend this to other times of the day, checking in with your breath. If you feel a sense of anxiousness, unease, stress, hold some time and space to simply breathe, tune in, feel where you are breathing from, allow your breath to ground, expand and rhythmically flow.

Our breath is our Connection to the Universe,
The field of Energy that is the Collective of Individuals
The Earth, her creatures and kingdoms that breathe and exchange the substance of life - Oxygen

Breathing is our substance of life, how we breathe and our relationship with our environment and others is imperative for our health and wellbeing

Today and every day;
- Find a space in nature, open your chest, let go, expand oneself and breathe to absorb the nourishment of nature and life.
- Breathe out and let go, feel the Earth underneath your feet supporting and holding you-let go of all your thoughts and fears

Affirmations:

"As I breathe, I breathe in my love of life"
"As I breathe, I breathe in the light of life, into every cell of my mind and body"

"I am free from all that serves me no purpose"
"I am free"
"I am grateful to be and to feel alive in this moment"
"I am Joy"
"I am Life itself"

I invite you to journal any thoughts, observations that came from doing the diaphragmatic breathing, how your body felt, what blocks there may have been, any releases and realisation.

14.

HOW OUR EMOTIONS ARE REFLECTED WITHIN OUR BODY

E-motion - Energy-In-Motion

Why do we have emotions?

Emotions are a product of thought, to enable us to act and mobilise the thought, an e-motion. They are there to stimulate the body to form a re-action, whether to run in flight or to fight, to speak, to protect, to reach out and hug someone, to procreate, to move to get warm, to eat.

As Charles Darwin proclaimed *"Emotions serve an adaptive role in our lives by motivating us to act quickly and take actions that will maximize our chances of survival and success."*

Our emotions form a chemical reaction within the limbic system of the brain, stimulating neurons to release neurotransmitters and neuropeptides, which stimulate and integrate the endocrine system and the nervous system, known as the neuroendocrine system. These form an activation of the required cells, tissues, organs and muscles in response to the emotion.

The limbic system includes the thalamus and hypothalamus that transforms emotions to physical responses. It is also involved in the production of important hormones for regulation of appetite, blood-sugar levels; body temperature and the autonomic functioning of the heart, lungs and the digestive and circulatory systems. The basal ganglia are for reward processing, habit formation, movement and learning.

The two major structures of the limbic system are the hippocampus and the amygdala.

The hippocampus is named after the scientific genius and is

recognised as the memory centre of our brains. Here, our episodic, associated memories are formed and catalogued, to be filed away in long-term storage across other parts of the cerebral cortex. These are long term memories that involve the recollection of specific events, situations, and experiences, such as memories of your first day of school, your first kiss, a special holiday.

Connections made in the hippocampus also help us associate memories with various senses, such as freshly cut grass is often associated with spring and summer, bringing joy and positivity. For some of us, this could also be a certain alcoholic drink that made you extremely ill years ago, yet the thought of the drink still forges the feeling of nausea to avoid the situation to happen again. This is where that connection is formed.

The hippocampus is important for spatial orientation and our ability to navigate the world and our environment. It is also one site in the brain where new neurons are made from adult stem cells. This process is called neurogenesis, and is the basis of one type of brain plasticity and "the roads of thought process", this is a key brain structure for learning new things.

Plasticity is the ability of the brain to change and adapt to new information. Synaptic plasticity is the change that occurs at synapses, the junctions and receptors between neurons that allow them to communicate.

The amygdala's is located right next to the hippocampus, the left and right amygdalae play a central role in our emotional responses, including feelings like pleasure, fear, anxiety and anger. The amygdala also attaches emotional content to our memories, and so plays an important role in determining how robustly those memories are stored.

Memories that have strong emotional meaning, with several senses tend to become ingrained, for instance, an experience of trauma, of feeling unsafe or vulnerable would be held here, allowing similar emotional experiences later in life to become a trigger of this deep rooted associated emotion.

The amygdala doesn't just modify the strength and emotional content of memories; it also plays a key role in forming new memories specifically related to fear. Fearful memories are then able to be formed after only a few repetitions, forming a repeating confirmation pattern of fear within our mind. It has recently confirmed by neuroscience researchers that new neurons are made in the amygdala.

Hence our brains will continue to create neural pathways of fear the more we trigger the sense of fear. Our brain thinks it as a thought, our mental energy, and if we attach to the thought and give it an emotional connection, this then creates neural activity, which stimulates the neuroendocrine system. These responsive hormones, which then connect to our visceral system, say the heart, liver, kidneys, depending on the emotion. This then travels back up through the Vagus Nerve, as 80% of its function is to send messages to the brain, which then tells the brain *"this is real!"*

However it isn't real, yet we continue the patterns and belief system, as once we have a belief, the brain seeks confirmation of such – thus we create our own reality from our own perception rather than truth!

The miracle comes when we become aware of this, and choose to change our perspective, to change our reality and to recognise we are worthy of greater things, of love, joy and peace in abundance!

How do our emotions affect our bodies?

Our glands, cells, tissues, organs and muscles all have receptors to receive these neuropeptides and neurotransmitters. The level of response and accumulation of these proteins and hormones within the cell and its nucleus, will depend on the emotion and its intensity.

For instance, a loving kind emotion that is expressed through a hug, or an intimate exchange, or supportive words, the emotion of love intensity released varies in its amplification sensation within our bodies. From a glow of happiness and joy, tears of joy of knowing one is loved, the sense of purpose and happiness felt knowing you are a creator of this joy in someone else, feeling of oneness, safety, security and support. It feels expansive within the heart area stimulating "happy hormones", serotonin, endorphins and oxytocin, which are fundamental to our health and wellbeing.

The greater the emotional amplitude, the greater the wave of sensation throughout the body.

The emotion and feeling of love is an open and expansive frequency and energy. The receptors of the cells become open to receive, allowing the flow of hormones and stimulus to process and release. These high emotions of love and joy are activating the parasympathetic nervous system, the foundation and nervous state of calm and stillness of mind, our digestion and immune system, healing and the act of procreation.

With the emotions of fear and anger, a different stimulus occurs; hormones such as cortisol are released via the activation of the sympathetic nervous system, stimulating the adrenals via the Hypothalamic Pituitary Adrenal Axis (HPA axis).

The focus of our energy is placed in increasing blood flow to serve the musculoskeletal system, enabling quick movement in a fight/flight response. Our vision becomes more tunneled, pupils dilate, our breath quickens to meet the demands of oxygen to convert to energy, the blood vessels vasodilate, blood clotting increases in case of injury, and the function and direction of energy is diverted away from the digestion system, as this is the lower priority when our safety is endangered.

These chains of reactions are fundamental to our survival when faced with potential danger; the body has reacted to the e-motion demands and starts the process of releasing the hormones that have served their purpose from the body, hence the need to urinate, the shaking and shivering of the body, crying.

We see it in the animal world, where an antelope narrowly escapes the jaws of a lion, shakes to remove this trauma and to then go back to its homeostasis and balance of grazing. Without this transition, the antelope would always be in a state of fear and would not be able to function to its optimum, it would cease grazing and would fatigue very quickly, which is what is happening to our bodies when our minds consciously or subconsciously are still in this state of fear or trauma.

This intrinsic release processes for us takes approximately 20-60 minutes to find its pre-arousal state of homeostasis, depending on the intensity of the situation. Imagine being woken up from your deep sleep with loud noises with the belief it was an intruder, to find it was the classic neighbour's cat, It would take you a while to fall back to sleep in this high emotional aroused state of being.

For a moment imagine how your day might be if this had happened, it may not be the most positive and productive day, probably feeling an element of irritation. The saying "getting off on the wrong foot", "got out the wrong side of the bed", and how this start seems to have seemingly one negative event after the other for that day and this is based upon a low scaled event.

As mentioned earlier, if certain events of fear and trauma are repeated it becomes stored within the amygdala, where neural pathways to the body, organs and cells have been formed. It is said that there is a fine line between the subconscious and the conscious; hence the brain is not always able to comprehend what reality actually is. Again, imagine yourself in a bad dream and you wake up from this, your heart is pounding, you are sweating, even nausea, the body has still reacted to this perceived threat, yet it was in your subconscious mind.

The bad dream may even cause a peculiar hangover of emotion, which lays within your persona and state of thought which you may even, though the event has not been "real", carry throughout the day, or until the hangover has subsided by distraction.

I remember having bad dreams of my boyfriend at the time now my husband, of him treating me badly or cheating on me, to then wake up and be in a bad mood with him, much to his undeserving astonishment. Which now writing this is making me chuckle out loud to myself, quite a lot, poor chap, however at the time I was most upset and it took a while to shift out this negative mood.

It can obviously happen in a positive way too, dreaming of pleasurable events and waking up to that physical state, say no more!

Reflecting on these bad dreams with what I know now, this was my subconscious bringing my deep rooted fears from my life's events and traumas, a narcissist relationship, to the surface of my conscious mind.

It may well have been a process to encourage the release of un-serving emotions, fears and thought patterns, to recognise them and to "shake it off" and become part of my healing. Although this understanding took time, the triggers were less often and formed part of my continuous growth and awareness of oneself.

Therefore, our primal fears and stresses of life are mainly our thoughts of the past and the future, not the present moment. Although they are not actually happening, the body will still react to these stimuli.

Say you are frustrated with a work colleague, becoming angry due to being unable to express your thoughts/emotions, with the feelings of being unsupported, unappreciated, or threatened; as the stressed environment is from thoughts of the mind rather than a physical fight/flight response, the body is not physically processing or releasing through movement or action, it is not "shaking off".

This restricts the transition back to the Parasympathetic Nervous System of homeostasis, the calm state. The body on a cellular level retains the neuropeptides/ transmitters and hormones in a constricted state, closing this cell from oxygenation and the fundamental metabolic process.

For a human cell to remain healthy, it needs to be open to allow oxygen and minerals to flow, like our breath; in with the essential supplies, and out with the removal of toxins and waste products through the metabolism of energy production.

These examples of situations may well be triggering old traumas, past events, thoughts and emotions that are stored within the amygdala, when you felt unsupported. When you were told or felt that were not good enough, in the school or home environment, or both, feeling humiliated, physically punished, feeling disempowered with no voice.

The neural pathways that have formed from the negative stimuli –thought- emotion- hormone-cell-organ, become recorded within the body, a pattern of thought, conscious or unconscious, laying a route similar to a road map.

These neural pathways become hyper sensitised, hyper-aroused from constant use forming deeper trenches, like tread marks on the road, it becomes the louder voice and negative stimulus in our bodies, feeding the cell to remain within the contracted state.

When the cell is contracted, it is affectively suffocated by the lack of oxygen and nutrients and the high level of toxicity. The cell closes and dehydrates, a "cutting off" from self, causing a chain of events, a ripple effect of tension and restrictions within the web of the fascia, developing to what eventually can be felt physically through pain and/or disease, over a prolonged period of time. We have become closed and disconnected from our cells and self, an inner loneliness!

Often these stresses or the feeling to release is through exercise, to clear one's mind and body, to work it off/out at the gym, which certainly supports the process on a physical level, although not always on the emotional; unless this is practiced with awareness, listening and observing one's thoughts and one's body's reaction.

Therefore as a preventative self-care, I truly believe we have to listen and observe our mind and bodies, a daily check in with oneself, ideally before the white flags and red flags appear, to prevent serious dis-ease. Yet, if these flags do present themselves, we are to see them as an opportunity, to make changes that serve you and your health. To hold this awareness and connection of mind and body, to release un-serving emotions, thought patterns and beliefs that have contracted and negatively affected our health.

If we consider these deep entrenched tyre tracks and well used roads in our psyche and bodies, we can see how easy it is to follow the same path in our lives, how challenges "dramas" are perceived in the same way, a reaffirming and feeding of the thought patterns that are ingrained within the limbic system.

Therefore, even with the intent of a different destination, the same roads and paths are used, like a scratch on a vinyl record, it gets stuck and cannot get past to listen to the rest of the song.

Hence the importance of self-care, self-awareness and observation, to recognise these repeating patterns and through visualisation reinforced by meditation, to connect with the limbic system, we begin to develop our neural plasticity, creating new positive neural pathways, streets and roads of open opportunities.

The effect of stress under the microscope-
It Damages Our Mitochondria!

Experiencing stress on a daily basis activates the fight-or-flight sympathetic nervous response in the body, which research has shown can damage the mitochondria in our cells, occurring commonly within the cells of the hippocampus and cortex, our limbic system.

The mitochondria are the powerhouse of the trillion of cells in our bodies; their health is intrinsic to ours, as they are vital for several metabolic pathways, including the Krebs cycle which is the production of ATP, our energy molecules.

They are also the key to lipid, cholesterol and hormone biosynthesis, as well as maintaining the cytosolic free calcium concentration within the cells, which has many cellular regularity functions, such as repair.

Free cytosolic calcium in turn serves as a cellular signal in divergent pathways, such as hormonal signaling. On the other hand, certain hormones exert their central endocrine action (directly or indirectly) via affecting mitochondrial function in various tissues and divergent cell-types.

When the mitochondria are damaged within its matrix, it causes the cellular DNA stored in the cell to break down into the rest of the cell, which eventually enters the bloodstream, acting similar to a hormone stimulating the endocrine system, causing an imbalance.

This intrinsic relationship of the mitochondria as the key to the endocrine system, a signaling feedback system of chemical messengers to internal glands, producing hormones to the relevant organs to function accordingly, highlights how detrimental stress can be on our health.

As the endocrine affects our whole mind and body, the symptoms of imbalance of organ dysfunction and the metabolic pathways are diverse, for instance yet not limited to, diabetes, chronic fatigue, fibromyalgia, ME, thyroid imbalance, prolonged transition of menopause.

Stress creates Myelin-Producing Cells – White Matter

Chronic stress and traumas can also lead to many long-term changes in your brain, as stress stimulates the production of myelin-producing cells.

Our brain is made up of neurons, axons, and support cells,

described as the grey and white matter. The grey matter includes our neurons which store and process information and support cells called glia.

The white matter is comprised of axons, which create a network of fibres that interconnect the neurons. The axons are surrounded by a white fatty myelin sheath, influencing the flow of electrical signals from cell to cell, for the communication of information. White matter acts similar to the conductor of the orchestra coordinating the interaction of the brain, when in balance, produces a beautiful harmony.

However, if you constantly feel stressed out, it can lead to an overproduction of myelin (white matter) and a reduction of neurons (grey matter), in some areas of the brain, which disrupts the delicate balance and timing of communication within the brain. Many brain abnormalities have been linked to imbalances in the white and grey matter of the brain.

The University of California, Berkeley, researchers have shown that chronic stress generates long-term changes in the brain, that may explain why people suffering chronic stress are prone to mental problems, such as anxiety and mood disorders later in life.

It is known that stress-related illnesses, such as post-traumatic stress disorder (PTSD), have abnormalities in the brain, including differences in the amount of grey versus white matter.

The studies were on one part of the brain, the hippocampus, providing insight into how white matter is changing in emotional imbalanced conditions, such as schizophrenia, autism, depression, suicide, ADHD and PTSD. It was concluded that PTSD patients could develop a stronger connectivity between the hippocampus and the amygdala, the core of the brain's fight or flight response, and lower than normal connectivity between the hippocampus and prefrontal cortex, which moderates our responses, our moments of reflection and awareness.

"You can imagine that if your amygdala and hippocampus are better connected, that could mean that your fear responses are much quicker, which is something you see in stress survivors. On the other hand, if your

connections are not so good to the prefrontal cortex, your ability to shut down responses is impaired. So, when you are in a stressful situation, the inhibitory pathways from the prefrontal cortex telling you not to get stressed don't work, as well as the amygdala shouting to the hippocampus, 'This is terrible!' You have a much bigger response than you should." –
Daniela Kaufer University of California, Berkeley

Imagine the conductor's main focus of the orchestra was the drums, the deep beat of fear, how this could overpower the harmony of the music, causing confusion and disarray of the rest of the orchestra, the lighter and higher frequencies of joy.

It was also found that stress also decreases the number of stem cells that mature into neurons, potentially providing an explanation for how chronic stress also affects learning and memory.

Stress Can Alter Your DNA

This is another significant impact of stress on a cellular level. As per research, environmental stress can bring about alterations in the genetic material within the nuclei of the cell. For example, one response to stress is that your fat-manufacturing genes become more active. This is a protective response to stress. However, in the long term, may lead to obesity and other related diseases.

Hopefully from this, you are able to conclude, that to improve your own health, mind and body, one needs to address the levels of stress in your life and body, be they present and/or past stresses and traumas, thus becoming the foundation to your healing journey.

With this understanding of the powerful and detrimental effect stress has on our health mind and body, to begin the process of empowerment and healing, one needs to look and reflect within, unpeel each layer or our being; we need to listen and observe our mind and body, with a more objective perspective.

Press the pause button; ask *"why am I stressed, why do I put myself under this stress, what am I trying to achieve, why do I feel I have to achieve, what are the triggers to this pressure and stress I place upon myself?"*

What are the narratives and the fears that lay within your mind, what is fuelling and driving your activity, do you feel you are not enough; do you believe to accomplish and feel complete and contented, can only be gained from a mystical element that is external to you? Have you been told that you are not enough, is this from your upbringing, is it social beliefs and systems?

How safe and supported do you feel, was there a time when you felt unsafe and unsupported, abandoned, rejected, lost, unloved? These levels vary subject to our experiences and the frequency of these emotions, that reaffirm in our fear-based control system in contrast to how much love, comfort and reassurance we have experienced throughout our lives.

What determines the intensity of our voices of fear is the balance of how much unconditional LOVE we hold for ourselves in our hearts and beings.

For us to achieve a healthier and happier mind and body, we need to have realistic views and goals for oneself. Being true to ourselves by looking inwards with honesty, and the realisation and acceptance of one's fears and negative thought patterns, which make us act the way we do; to make small positive steps to change them, towards holding pure unconditional love for you, within you.

Reaffirm to oneself every day

"I am ENOUGH, I am LOVE and LOVED
I am SUPPORTED, I am SAFE
I choose LOVE-JOY-PEACE
I am WORTHY OF LOVE-JOY-PEACE
I am LOVE- I am JOY- I am PEACE

Say these affirmations our loud, let them become the louder voice in the room, change and redirect these neural pathways within your mind and body.

Be aware of what voices that may come up which are in conflict to these positive vibes, this is your BS. (Belief systems or bull-shite, whichever you prefer – I prefer the latter, it tends to call it out more!)

15.

HOW MEDITATION AFFECTS OUR MIND

Communication of neurons within our brain is displayed through our emotions, thoughts and behaviour. As communication occurs, brainwaves are released by synchronised electrical pulses or oscillations.

Brainwaves create our "state of being" that enhance our individual mental focus, activation of the sympathetic and parasympathetic nervous system.

These brainwaves are measured at different frequencies;

Beta 12-38Hz – This is typically when we are in an alert state of mind, a waking activity, stimulation of the sympathetic nervous system, which is natural and required when we wake up, to start the necessary functioning of the body. It is the higher Beta waves 20hz upwards, when we are within a higher stress alert consciousness.

Alpha- 8-12Hz – when we are physically and mentally relaxed in a safe and loving environment, being more in the present moment, our parasympathetic nervous system. It is an awake yet relaxed state of mind, the base rhythm of the human brain and is more predominant when our eyes are closed.

In this frequency, we become more creative due to the expansion of the brain and neurons, reducing negative thoughts due to the stimulation of our feel good hormones from love, for example oxytocin and serotonin.

When alpha wave oscillations are more prominent, sensory input minimises the mind, generally releasing unwanted thoughts and the dominant presence of this rhythm is a necessary pre-condition to enter into a meditation. When the brain shifts into more thought, the alpha oscillations reduce and transitions into the higher frequency of Beta.

Theta Waves- 4-8Hz which encompasses the Earth's Magnetic Field, the Schumann Resonance 7.8Hz. These brainwaves are experienced when we are in deep sleep or in meditation. When within this frequency of our mind, it becomes the gateway to the subconscious, focusing internally without awareness of the surrounding environment. Vivid mental imagery occurs and through theta healing, it creates space for physical healing and re-programming of the subconscious beliefs and positive manifestation, which is used in hypnosis.

Interestingly, meditation has been linked to larger amounts of grey matter in the hippocampus and frontal areas of the brain. An increase of grey matter and neural pathways can lead to more positive emotions, longer-lasting emotional stability and heightened focus during daily life.

Trials have also showed that routine meditative practice is associated with a long-lasting change in the topology of definite brain areas, suggesting that meditation might be able to induce brain plasticity, our adaptive mind – in other words, we can change our reality and the perception of it, we can change our neural pathways, our whole body and being overtime!

So when we say out loud or to ourselves things like, *"this is me, I am too old to change"*, this is simply BS, because you can change, should you choose and desire to! And quite frankly, from after reading this, and you still say these things and believe it- this may well be a story you tell yourself, because you have become too scared of the unknown! If so, hold compassion not judgement - *Tough love right there Dear Soul x*

A study was conducted to understand if Mindfulness Meditation is related to long-lasting changes in the Hippocampus during the resting state, using magneto-encephalography (MEG) technology, a neuroimaging technique for mapping brain activity.

"In the light of the functional role of the right hippocampus and its

activation in the theta band, our results indicate that meditation might have functional effects on prospective and spatial memories. These findings suggest that meditation, if constantly practiced, could be a candidate as a non-pharmacological intervention in pathologies characterized by alteration in the hippocampal areas"

https://pmc.ncbi.nlm.nih.gov/articles/PMC6312586/

Delta Waves – 0.5-4hz - are mostly predominant when in 4th stage of sleep, which is when we are at our deepest. When delta waves are present, the body is at its most relaxed, thus reducing stress and have been shown to reduce cortisol within our bodies.

Delta waves can also be stimulated through certain frequency bi-neural beats at 432hz; also through gentle touch to the palms of the hands, face and upper arms, which highlights the power of touch from the somatic stimuli to our nervous system.

Delta waves are healing to the body, however when Delta waves are present when fully awake, these may be representational of possible ADHD, brain lesions and Alzheimer's, as well as high toxicity within the brain/blood barrier from chemicals, heavy metals – much more research is needed here!

For me this shows a dis-coherence of mind and body, where the neural systems are not communicating as one, nor relating to the environment and stimuli. Possible contributing factors such as stress, lack of grounding to Earth, the gut-brain and blood-brain barriers weakened through chemicals and heavy metals in food, household products, to pharmaceutical drugs.

Promoting a good sleep protocol is fundamental to our health – for example, beginning with meditation to clear the mind, to find a higher perspective and reduce stress; Epsom salt baths with lavender – feeds our body with magnesium that is intrinsic to relaxation; to be in sleep by 11pm; no stimuli such as caffeine and alcohol, no blue light from our screens, and not eating late will help the body rest and restore.

Gamma Waves – 38-100hz and the highest type known as hypergamma, which are associated with emotional states of compassion and unconditional love; when the brain activity involves simultaneous processing of information from different areas of the brain, with high cognitive functionality, memory recall and learning. In this wave, you are able to learn languages more easily, experience happiness more frequently, yet also experience no mental activity, where the mind becomes one, a unity and witnessing state – we become the observer and one at the same time!

You may wish to read into Nirvikalpa Samadhi and Ken Wilber to explore more about this state of being. You may also find this in the meditations I channel – many have shared with me, a state and sense of oneness and peace when listening to these guided meditations and visualisation journeys, as well as in my 1:1 hands on sessions.

In summary and my opinion, meditation is a beautiful form alongside breath work, to connect one's mind and body. To expand one's mind, creating new neural pathways and roads of thought, away from the repetitive fear based memories, which trigger our daily thoughts and stress, directly influencing the level of our health and wellbeing.

The fact that meditation increases grey matter and cognitive thought; reducing the sensitive and the emotional responses pathways of fear (the amygdala), and improves our mood, it is within no doubt in my mind that, meditation and breath work is a free intrinsic self-care tool.

We can tap into and build our practice, to support us in what we are seeing as a decline in mental wellbeing, increased neural diversity, brain fog, and neural degenerative diseases such as Alzheimer's (aka Stage 3 Type diabetes – this is an insulin resistant disease!).

The chapter, *Pineal Gland-The Magick Bean* will open your awareness to this even more!

Meditation also is a foundation to beholding and embodying a higher perspective in life, to become aware and the observer of self, *"to know thyself"*- inscribed at the Oracles of Delphi, and later other religious equivalents, translation and interpreted meaning.

To "see", to be conscious of our ego, our subconscious,

unconscious beliefs and patterns; quite like a hall of mirrors, that either become confusion or a pathway to our truth. To even question what we perceive as our truth, that our truth may actually be fluid, are we our thoughts, or are our thoughts us, and where do our thoughts come from?

    This is when heart and mind coherence come into play, for this feels like a game of ping pong of the mind, this coherence balances the mind, the pre-frontal cortex, our emotional intelligence, seen in improved and steady Heart Rate Variability (HRV). For I believe our heart, a torus field that is the grounding force of Mind, Body, Soul and Spirit as one, our truth is felt here, when we have connected to and embodied unconditional love within.

16.

THE CHAKRAS
Unpeeling the emotional and physical layers through the energy systems of our bodies

What sustains life itself?

I do not proclaim to be a quantum physician nor biologist to any degree, however, I have an absolute fascination as to how our body is here on planet Earth, and how it functions in balance and homeostasis with nature.

When we look through a microscope so deeply and intensified through the layers of our physical, we see our cells, the mitochondria, the power house of our cells, deeper still we see the energy, the light within our cells and being, our nerves connect through light receptors.

As we come through and see light from a micro level, we enter a gateway and open into a macro vision of life, that light is the creator of life itself, it is the source to all living things on our planet. With this in mind you could say we are all one of the same source, we are a collective of energy connected to the same life force that creates and sustains us.

Going further, we could see how our own individual frequency of thoughts and actions influence this source of life within us. Forming an imprint within this universal energy and light, interacting with all all that is connected to this energy - our life force, the collective of all living things.

We are a beacon and transmitter of frequencies interacting with this field of light. We, through this creation of life, our bio-fields, underneath our skin, our physical body and cells, are all one of the same, a united collective of one!

It certainly gets the grey matter flexing, crumbling old belief and thought processes, and opening the mind that we are not just individuals in our own world, going about our own business, being in complete control of our universe.

In fact, it is the reverse, we are all affecting one another directly and indirectly, we are co-creators of our life and the universe, and to function to our optimum of health and happiness we need to resonate to an infinite, expansive and connective energy, supporting one another, aka unconditional love!

Our Energy Fields and Chakras

We are alive because of the life force that is flowing through us, known as Chi, Ki, Prana, detailed in many ancient text and Sanskrit thousands of years ago. The life force flows within the physical body through pathways referred to as Chakras, Meridians and Nadis, flowing around the whole body as a field of energy called an Aura, nourishing the organs and cells of the body, supporting them in their vital functions.

Knowing that our plains of emotions hold different frequencies, be they contracted through shame, fear and anger, or open and expansive through gratitude, love and joy - we can come to understand that our emotions affect the energy bio-field that sustains our bodies.

Over the last five thousand years, Chakras have been recognised by sages, mystic, philosophers, the seers of India, and described as subtle energies in our environment and bodies in various ways.

When two dynamic energies within nature combine they form a spiral, a spinning pattern or vortices. We see this in many scales, ranging from tiny spiral eddies on the surfaces of river and streams to powerful whirlpools, even in space we see a galaxy forming in a spiral, the movement and cloud formations create cyclones and anticyclones; the beautiful display of auroras, also known as the northern and southern lights.

All living plants, creatures, including humans, are a creation by Mother Earth and are sustained through this intrinsic relationship of the elements, earth, water, fire-sun and air. Our chakras are the energy centres of our body relating to these elements, they are a complex set of energy interactions that become denser in energy to form our physical human mind, body and spirit.

They are gateways to our physical and emotional body, forming channels of communication and flow, allowing the life force, our energy and light to flow within our bodies. Any energetic imbalances through the emotional and physical, forms dysfunction, becoming a restriction of flow!

There are seven main chakras of the body that have physical correspondences, starting from the base of our bodies, our feet and lower limbs to the crown of our head. In Ancient texts, the chakra and nadis are considered expressions of consciousness; they are not bound by the laws of matter, as they are energy, the three dimensional physical relationship is a way of understanding in familiar terms.

Similar to viewing a square as 2D, the cube as 3D, a Tesseract as 4D and hypercube as 5D, all are an expansion and laying of one another, depending on one's perspective and way of viewing!

Or the Vesica Piscis, two intertwined circles, as they spin they become a torus, which from another perspective displays the seed of life – and most interestingly, the electromagnetic field around us, our heart and blood vessels are shaped as a toroid- a torus!

There are other chakras that extend from these seven chakras, namely the Earth Star, Cosmic Star and Stellar Gateway, which root-hold us within the Earth and the Universe, however the main seven will be explored in this book.

Around each chakra system emanating its function are one of the main endocrine glands, our hormone system, which is intrinsically linked to the limbic system, our thoughts and emotional centre; a plexus of nerves and concentration of blood vessels and lymph nodes.

It is thought that the life force originates from the root, our base chakra from conception, developing through our chakra, the key stages and milestones of life to adulthood at the Crown.

Once completed the whole cycle of the seven chakras, the process begins again with the base chakra and can repeat itself many times over in a life time, giving us the opportunity to heal and repair ourselves, to strengthen our energy within the chakra system expressing our full potential.

For example, the Crown chakra becomes active between 20-27 years of age as we fully interact with the world, which corresponds with the fact that our brains are not fully developed until we are circa 28 years old! - The chakra relates to questions like *"Why am I here, is there more to life than this"?* Which can remain dormant or denied at this age, yet this returns circa the age of 40, when these questions if denied previously, become more prevalent, seeking change and purpose of life, often seen and described as a mid-life crisis!

Interestingly, in the reverse, studies have shown that when someone passes away, the chakras and energy systems close from the base, sacral and solar plexus, the pattern of the energy flow as the person nears death becomes thin and draws in towards the physical body, and the chakras close from the feet upward, leaving through the heart and/or crown.

17.

BASE CHAKRA -MULADHARA "ROOT"
"I am Safe and Supported"

Overview

The base chakra Muladhara, which means root in Sanskrit, it is our foundation of life in the physical body with the ability to sustain life itself and it is the closest energy centre to Earth and links us to the planet.

It is the support of our physical earthly existence, represented by the element of the Earth and the colour red. It connects us in a downward opening energy from our genitals to the Earth Star that is situated within the Earth 15-20 cm below our feet. The Earth star is our sacred space of magick, mystery, gifts and talents held within the wisdom of the Earth.

The chakra is represented by the deep Earthly colours of red. Red is the colour of fire and blood, it is associated with strong outward and visible energy, strength and power, determination as well as passion, desire, and love. Dark red is associated with vigor, willpower, leadership and courage.

Reddish brown to copper is the representation of the Earth Star. Copper conducts electrical impulses and magnifies energy. I see this as our connection to the earth and the transferring of energy, the grounding of the electro-magnetic torus field, the energetic exchange of what we give to the earth and how the Earth supports us. Interestingly, Copper can combat lethargy, passivity, restlessness, excitability, and non-acceptance of oneself. It stimulates initiative, optimism, diplomacy and independence.

The Cycle of Nature and Development–

The base chakra is about our anchoring into the physical world from conception, birth to 1 year old, our "foundation" years.

As the chakras go through each cycle as we grow, the base chakra is also about taking up our space in the world, to claim our sovereignty, our Divinity and to know that our presence is a gift to the world, to be fully embodied in our talents, gifts and wisdom, as a deep sense of purpose and connection.

It gives us presence, visibility, a vibration and frequency to be seen heard and felt. When we feel safe and supported within ourselves, our body, our heart, our truth, we are able to expand our presence, our heart torus field, fully grounded within the Earth, which the base chakra embodies and supports as a whole.

Physically-

The chakra relates and encompasses the lower limbs from the soles of the feet to the hips and the whole musculoskeletal system, to have solidarity and integrity to hold and support with flexibility and strength.

The endocrine systems related to the base chakra are the adrenal glands, which have an intrinsic relationship with the Hypothalamic Pituitary Adrenal (HPA) Axis, which releases cortisol, the stress hormone. The axis affects the circulatory system producing heat, our thermoregulatory function, inflammation and can manifest as anxiety, as well as these other symptoms of adrenal imbalance:

- Persistent unexplained fatigue.
- Waking un-refreshed after a good night's sleep.
- Brain fog.
- Impaired memory.
- Muscle aches and joint pains.
- Tiring easily after minor exertion.
- Decreased capacity to handle stress.
- Mild depression.

The organs specific to the base chakra are the bladder, kidneys and prostrate.

The nervous system includes the coccygeal plexus and the sciatic nerve, which runs from the buttocks to the soles of the feet. I have found through many clients, any impact of the coccyx area can have a lasting effect of shock absorbed within the Dura of the central nervous system, and sometimes into the liver and kidneys, which are also the body's shock absorbers, emotionally and physically! The result is that the Dura tube which envelopes the whole central nervous systems, shrinks in dehydration as tension, similar to a coiled spring, thus placing stress on the nervous system.

Emotionally-

The base chakra is about feeling safe and secure in all aspects of your life, to feel supported and to trust this support, from our physically environment, health to our finances, including our emotional environment in our personal and work life.

The question that runs through the base chakra is "Am I Safe and Am I Supported?", which then supports all of the other chakras to be balanced. Am I safe to express my desires (sacral)?; Am I safe to take action (solar plexus)?; Am I safe to love and be loved (heart)?, Am I safe to express and be in my truth (throat)?: It then supports our mind to be of high consciousness, to become an observer of self - Are my thoughts of fear or love (third eye)? For then our choices to be of awareness and greater intention (crown), which completes the cycle as whole.

Balance and optimum flow –

When the chakra emotionally and physically is open, we are in balance with our sense of self and the desire to live our roots to our existence; this is the ground of our being that sustains us.

We feel supported and safe to make decisions that feel aligned with our needs and heart desires; we trust ourselves and take each step of life with courage and curiosity.

Imbalance symptoms-

When we place too much value and emphasis of control and to know, rather than our inner knowing and feeling, creates an imbalance, relying on our mind and the need to know rather than a calm state of acceptance and trust

We have a disassociation with the physical reality and a sense of being creates disdain, detachment and life becomes dull and meaningless, a *"what is the point?!"* attitude and mind-set. Life feels hard and an outward struggle, with a belief that if anything needs to be done, *"you have to do it yourself"*, and mostly likely holds a distrust of others consciously and/or subconsciously; one generally does everything themselves rather than asking for support and help. This is also recognised as survival behaviour of childhood trauma, not asking for help or receiving help and being fiercely independent!

When imbalanced it manifests as restrictions and tensions of the musculoskeletal system, primarily the lower limbs and lower back, however the whole body overtime due to compensation.

Depending on whether the emotion/thought patterns relates more of the feminine or masculine, will determine the predominant side of restrictions felt.

Left the feminine (female-mother-past); right, the masculine (male-father-future). What blocks us from moving with ease and grace, what are the thought patterns of restrictions, the past experiences, fears of moving forward and of change; a resistance to being in the feminine "being" energy, and too much in one's masculine "doing" energy; the over control and being "ahead" of oneself; spending too much time in the future worries rather than being in the present; not feeling supported by one's close relationships, parents, partners?

Imbalance is also experienced as mood swings, stress, anxiety and depression, often feel overwhelmed, finding it hard to concentrate; hormone imbalance and conditions of inflammation and a lack of energy; frequent physical health issues; on-going financial "perceived" concerns and often fearful of the unknown, preferring to know and plan/control as many aspects of life.

Ankle and inflexibility of the lower limbs represent the feeling of being unsupported, mentally ahead of oneself from over worry and concern. The head tips over the plumb line (the central line to measure your posture), contracting the posterior fascia chain of connective tissues, muscles, ligaments and tendons, the back of the legs including the sciatic nerve, all the way up to the back of the neck, the occiput, including the spinal postural muscles to prevent us from falling forward and over ourselves.

The facial chain becomes contracted and fatigued. Often seen as tight hip flexor muscles that tilt the pelvis, antagonising the posterior back muscles from the sacral to occiput and then distally to the limbs including the hamstrings, gastrocnemius (calves) and plantar fascia, also creating tension in the gluteus group and piriformis (buttocks) and the sciatic nerve.

I see this in client's postures, where the head is ahead of the plumb line, with protracted shoulders (hunched), which in time become curvature of the spine. The general energy and mental energy, is keeping oneself small, keeping one's head down, not taking up the space they deserve and are worthy of. To remedy this, would be to feel safe, and be present as one's full self, as they love and accept themselves. Safe to be seen, to holds one's head high and in an ease and grace, to see the full horizon and to trust the future!

Due to the base chakra's link to the HPA axis, that has very similar symptoms to what we see detailed in perimenopause and menopause. Stress significantly impacts the adrenal glands, and as oestrogen productions shifts to the these glands from the ovaries, there is a conflict, a toxic cocktail, that may as producing a growth hormone actually be a cause for cancer.

I believe at this pinnacle time of life, as one is transitioning from Mother to Wise One, women are being called to go through a complete change of beliefs, patterns and ways of being, to truly step up and into their power. To slow down with more ease and grace into their feminine energy, however, they have to become conscious of the subconscious and unconscious which has them out of alignment, of their desires, pleasure and power, in the over-doing. To find healthy boundaries and express them, to no longer over-give and martyr one's energy, like a clapped out Cinderella!

Oestrogen levels are dropping significantly because of the high levels of stress and environmental factors, my belief is that the true healing comes from seeking the root of the stress, rather than simply taking fake hormones and continuing the ways of being, that no longer serve you neither joy nor purpose!

(Feel this will be my second book, thinking I'll call it Pussy Power!)
"*I trust and surrender to the absolute support of the universe*"

The base chakra Muladhara, which means root in Sanskrit; it is our foundation of life in the physical body with the ability to sustain life itself and it is the closest energy centre to Earth and links us to the planet.

For us to access our wisdom, talents and gifts, first we must be grounded and centred, to feel safe, so we are able to transition from survival to thriving. When we are thriving and grounded we are accessing our power and abilities to create and manifest, bringing our dreams into our reality.

"A seed may lay within the Earth for eons, until the right moment and environment presents itself, an environment that embodies trust and growth"

When we think about a new-born baby's first action is to feel supported, belonging and cared for, when placed upon the mother's chest when born, the babies instinctive action is to "root" for the mother's breast, to feed, to feel their mother's heartbeat that has been there since conception, their "known", to find reassurance and to feel safe in this new world.

To say the baby is really thriving, it is because all their needs are being met, they feel safe, loved and nurtured. This continues into our adult life with more conscious and subconscious stresses of money how, safe and supported we feel and are our needs being met, are we loved, heard and acknowledged?

However as an adult, we must recognise that the power to fulfill these needs are within us, we are no longer "dependent" on others to survive, we are able to choose thriving over surviving and the power of this, is our choice in conscious awareness, *this beautiful Souls, is your Empowerment.*

When we "cut the cords" we become an independent Soul on our own journey, free from the stories of the past and our ancestral lineage. We break the patterns of the fear, our encoded emotional and physical DNA, yet we have the ability to change our genome expression by our chosen frequency of how we wish to feel, see and be in this world, to be able to stand proudly, comfortably and fully embodied on our own two feet.

Imbalances of the base chakra may originate from conception, the health and wellbeing of our Mother's, how safe she felt and her emotionally state. All would have been transferred to us on some level through the blood that flows between mother and child whilst in the womb. I have had clients where their pain is shown to be emotional pain, such as betrayal, held within the liver and heart, that was their Mother's experience, when pregnant with the client, yet also when the Mother was a child herself.

Science is finally recognising what we call "ancestral trauma", the mitochondria that comes only from the Mother, can hold trauma of over 50 generations, I believe it goes back to whenever we began and when trauma occurred, as energetic encoding in our blood and bones, our deep unconscious body.

How we are born and any complications at our birth, be that a vaginal birth, breech, C-section, whether we were united with our Mother straight away, and how quickly the umbilical cord was cut, all have an impact in our central nervous system and musculoskeletal system.

Any restrictions from what is naturally a traumatic experience, even if it "went well", will affect us, and are held within our bodies, the connective tissue, the fascia, and as we grow, we grow with these tensions, unless treated.

Through our early foundation and development stages, as we are little energetic sponges to our external environment, our brains are in Theta wave, receiving and imprinting into our subconscious mind, there is no discernment of what is ours and what is other's, our parents and guardians.

We absorb and take on others beliefs and patterns as our own, held within our subconscious, they simply become a pattern that we are unaware of, until we choose to hold space in an objective awareness of self, to begin the process of "learning the unlearning".

To Survive or Thrive that is the Question?!

The base chakra first layer is survival and to survive well, a level of practicality and support, it relates to our whole musculoskeletal system with the main physical aspect from the soles of the feet to the hips; to hold an integrity and strength to allow the body to be present and the space for each organ, cell, tissue to flow; any compression and restriction would block this natural energetic flow, known as "chi", our life force.

The base chakra I see as our masculine energy, male or female, to be present, to be seen and the integrity which supports our boundaries. To embody and to retain our sovereignty, our life force, our power within, it is the structure, the helix that enables our feminine energy of creativity and joy, which relates to our sacral chakra, to be expressed and flow, giving life and oxygen to every cell of our body and mind.

Physically, the base chakra encompasses the coccygeal nerve plexus, which alongside the sacral nerves, provides sensory innervation of the skin in the coccygeal region. Delivering sensory and motor innervation to their respective dermatomes and myotomes, with partial innervation to several pelvic organs, including the womb, fallopian tubes, bladder, and prostate, our organs of creativity, pleasure and joy.

The base chakra represents the adrenal system, that responds physically, emotionally and energetically to the condition and tension of our pelvic floor muscles and the perineum, the area between the anus and yoni (vagina) in females, or in males the anus to penis, which form part of the deep frontal line of fascia and vice versa.

This fascia forms part of the Deep Front line that incorporates deep roots under the foot, the skeleton of the back leg, behind the knee and inner thigh, through the hip, pelvis and the front of the lumbar vertebrae, connecting to an additional line that runs through the back of the thigh to the pelvic floor and back to the first lumbar vertebrae.

It continues upward through the diaphragm, chest, the thoracic viscera and ends on the bottom of both the neuro-cranium and the visceral cranium.

The fascia line takes on a deep strength and supportive role of our skeletal and visceral system. If tight, it draws the body in a fetal position in extreme, which we would form into in moments of traumatic stress as a way to protect our most vulnerable aspects of ourselves, our organs.

This would often be seen with a tight psoas (hip flexor), also known as the "Seat of the Soul". In Buddhist traditions, the psoas is said to store trauma and emotionally charged tension, playing a key role in our fight or flight, or freeze response.

There are two muscles either side of the lumbar spine, across the pelvis and into the groin, head of the femur (thigh bone). It is the deepest muscle in the body and the only muscle that connects the torso to the legs. It flexes the trunk towards the legs (as in squatting), supports the abdominal organs and acts as a pump driving fluids such as lymph and blood in and out of body cells. It has a key relationship with breathing as it connects through the fascia to the diaphragm; any tension in the psoas can affect from how we walk to how we breathe and how much space we take up in this world.

Hence a fear of standing our ground, being seen, judged and even persecuted may reside in tight hip flexors.

Neuroendocrine

In direct relationship, any stimulation emotional or physically will be fed through the neuroendocrine system, our Hypothalamic Pituitary Adrenal (HPA) axis and the cranial nerve, the Vagus Nerve (CNX); from the bladder to the autonomic nervous system, creating a hormonal and neural waves of responses.

If in fear, it will channel via the Sympathetic Nervous System which forms part of our fight/flight or freeze response, or if joy and pleasure it stimulates the parasympathetic nervous system, our rest digest, feed and breed.

Hence we cannot be in joy and thriving mode when our survival needs are being triggered, either through not being met, our perception of, and our fear of them not being so.

Should our bodies be holding conscious and subconscious stress, our deep frontal line will be tight and draw us inwards and downward, a curling into self, our shoulders inward, our head forward and our eye line dropping down.

For a moment, accentuate this in your body, how does this feel, do you feel confident and vibrant full of energy and confidence to step up an into the world, with focus and clarity on what you have in your mind, goals and desires; or do you feel like dropping in and shying away, what emotions come up for you, sadness, grief, hopelessness?

Now do the opposite, hold your core, soften your feet and the back of your knees, roll your shoulder back and look to the horizon, now breathe into your belly and heart. Be mindful of your emotional states when you change your physical and vice versa.

"I am where I belong"

When stressed and in survival mode, the mind and body are always communicating via the network of nerves and arterial, and one of the primary aspects is to know what type of surface one is on. To know what level of effort would be required should the actual fight/flight response be necessary, the mind is in direct communication with the feet and the lower part of the body and vice versa.

These emotional and chemical responses heightens and stimulates the Sympathetic Nervous System(SNS), the adrenals which are linked to the mind through the Hypothalamic Pituitary Adrenal (HPA) Axis, our central stress response system - an eloquent and ever-dynamic intertwining of the central nervous system and endocrine system.

Very rarely are we actually in a situation or environment that challenges our survival, yet the subconscious emotional imbalance constantly feeds and stimulates this intricate communication system.

Overtime, we can see this stress being physically being represented in our bodies, the lower limbs, tensions and restrictions form with a lack of flexibility of the toes, feet, ankles, knees, hips and the lower back, which are the foundation and support of our bodies.

Without flexibility, shock absorption is lowered and the impact has a ripple and stress affect throughout the whole musculoskeletal system and soft tissues. The body starts to compensate, shortening, tilting and rotating to enable the body to still function and move, yet on a more restricted basis.

These structural shifts of imbalance tightens and dehydrates the fascia, the connective tissue from the skin to the cellular level, causing fatigue, heat and inflammation, inhibiting the metabolic process within the affected and restricted cells. The visceral systems lay within and is protected and supported through the musculoskeletal system, which supports the nerves, arterial, lymph supply and circulation, thus any imbalance will have a direct affect to the optimum function of our organs and vice versa.

"I am Safe and I am Supported"

The overloaded effect on the neuroendocrine system via the adrenals, which form part of the base chakra, increases the cortisol levels within our body; reducing activation of the cranial vagus nerve, the parasympathetic nervous system, causing a depletion of the digestion and immune system and further inflammation and constriction to a cellular level. Inflammation is seen as heat, friction in the body links to symptoms that have "itis" in their name, e.g. arthritis, rheumatoid arthritis, colitis etc.

As the adrenals sit above the kidneys, they have a direct affect to the function of the kidneys, thus in turn via the ureter to the bladder.

Any symptoms that are associated to the kidneys would be related to the base chakra, for instance oedema, levels of toxicity, uric acid, gout, bladder infections, irritation, pain and incontinence.

Stating that one needs to work from the base chakra, our foundation and the emotions that stimulate the physical response first would be an understatement! The health of all of the other chakras, our emotional and physical body rely on the support and balance from our connection with the Earth; through our lower limbs, to trust and feel supported, to feel safe and that one belongs here.

I invite you to note any thoughts, understandings, aha moments...

18.

THE SACRAL CHAKRA – SVADISTANA – "SWEETNESS"
"I Choose Joy, I am Worthy of Joy, I am Joy"

Overview

The Sacral Chakra is the representation of the sweetness of life, our joy, sensuality, passion and desires, as our purpose in this world is joy!

The energetic centre links to the element of water, and as water carries all knowledge and memory of what it has touched; it is our centre of deep inner wisdom of the Earth. She is the flow and energy to create and bring abundance and growth.

The waves of our oceans expand and contract and flow from the power and connection of our moon, it is our darker and deeper aspect of us, for the moon has greater presence in the light of the dark skies.

The sacral chakra holds a deep feminine energy and power, which like water can be gentle yet also most powerful. The connection of the moon and water influences women's hormones and menstrual cycle, any irregularity the sacral chakra is calling for healing.

The sacral chakra is our emotional centre that needs to be in a constant flow to ensure vibrancy rather than stagnancy. The stages and cycles of the moon through the effects of water affect our emotional states and are most powerful when we consciously connect, to be in a flow to release and manifest our desires.

The energy centre is represented by the colour orange. Orange combines the energy of red with the happiness of yellow. It is associated with joy, sunshine, and the tropics. Orange represents enthusiasm, fascination, happiness, creativity, determination, attraction, success, encouragement. Represented by the wonderful glow of the sun, in sunsets and sunrises, when its intensity has reduced so it can be observed and enjoyed.

Cycle of Nature and development- growing from the foundation years of the root chakra, the energy centres merge and integrate from around 6 months to 2 years of age.

Physical representation -The sacral chakra encompasses the pelvic area, the hips and sacroiliac joint; the bladder which also links to the base chakra via the adrenal and kidneys, it is the organ of emotional release; the reproductive organs are centres of creativity, pleasure and sensuality.

For women, when menstruating, it is also an opportunity to release deep emotions through the blood and the water within, hence the often heightened emotions and sensitivity. This process of release also includes the large intestines, the final embodiment of discernment – the absorption of what serves and the release of what no longer serves joy or purpose, where forgiveness and a space of acceptance is needed to let go.

The nerves within are the sacral nerve plexus, which innervate the pelvic and reproductive organs, and the soft tissues including the buttocks and perineum; they also have a connection to the sciatic nerve via the sacrum.

The sacral chakra links to the neuroendocrine limbic system the emotional control centre of our mind, through the essence of water.

When we breathe deeply, our sacral bone moves anteriorly and posteriorly, acting like a paddle-wave generator to encourage the flow of the Cerebrospinal Fluid.

Keeping an open and flexible sacral chakra-sacrum stops stagnancy, a lethargy and toxicity build up, physically, emotionally, mentally and energetically.

Balance and optimum flow – When the sacral chakra is in balance and flow, you have waves of feeling tenderness, joy and bliss. You love to be creative and can go with the flow in the changes of life. You are able to express your emotions well and are able to move on easily. Your mind is flexible and your body has a comfortable strength and flexibility within the pelvis and lower limbs.

Imbalance symptoms- If unbalanced the sacral chakra will physical represent in lack of/ or intense levels of libido; fertility issues; irregular menstrual cycles including heavy and painful periods, erectile issues, irritable bowel syndrome, inflammation and bloated lower abdominal area; oedema, poor circulation to the lower limbs. I have also seen extended to the upper limbs and in Reynard's Disease; bladder control and infections, poor mineral absorption, fatigue, lower back pain, often referring down to the sciatic nerve.

You have a tendency to resist the flow of sweetness of life and energy, often shutting down, and life feels dull lacking vibrancy and colour. A suppression and shut down of your sexual energy and expression of self, becoming disconnected from self and life. Like a dam, closed off creating a huge pressure and prolapse of organs within the pelvic area, such as bladder control, yet also no water, a drought, so dry and itchy which may also extend to the eyes, as the suppression of the expression and release of emotions.

Or, if over energised and open, you have addictive behaviours, a craving for sweetness, sugar, sex, alcohol like a tsunami, a lot of drama in self with mood swings, and all can become too much and feel overwhelmed.

Life is Sweet

This is where we hold the Svadistana, the sweetness and pleasure of life, to be in touch and flow with our emotions, our emotional, sexual wellbeing, passion, desire and sensuality.

It is the centre of rebirth and creation, to be able to create the miracle of life itself, to bring life to projects that bring joy and a higher purpose to society. The chakra relates to the element of water, which supports the abundance and creation of life, it is our centre for creativity and joy to flow in abundance.

It has the power to recreate, or more so, to truly reveal ourselves in our truth and expression, our inner blueprint, when in balance with the throat and heart chakra. Our throat and genitals are connected through the fascia, the deep frontal line, which envelopes the spine energetically, which is felt like a cylinder of light from your groin, perineum and anus to your throat.

Working this energetically through intention, visualisation and breath work, is what I call flossing this deep sacred tube of connection – our connection to our truth, desires and integrity. It also improves our sensitivity and ability to orgasm; add in self-pleasure and you may find increased connection and intensity, clearing out any blocked emotions through the throat, and expansion within the mind and crown. Give yourself the permission to explore, be curious and play, and make as much noise as you wish, as this is great on so many levels!

Our sacral chakra cycle of nature and development activates consciously from around six months to two years old. The feedback comes from pleasure and gratification. The distinction between mother and child becomes more apparent, allowing the child to explore and experience without negativity and reprimand, building confidence as an individual, to explore and learn.

Once the baby's primal survival needs have been assured, the baby then explores through play, their surroundings and environment, forming an understanding of the potential of their body developing and using all of the senses. As the cycle returns through our lives, it is about recognising our uniqueness, our gifts and creativity, to explore, to experience the pleasure, joy and our flow in life.

The chakra is located in the area below the navel, the lower back and sacrum know in Greek times, "the Holy Bone" and above the pubic bone. It physically relates to the hollow organs within the pelvis and lower abdominal area – the large intestine and sigmoid colon, the bladder and the reproductive organs. It represents the sacroiliac joint which includes the sacrum, pelvis and lower back of the musculoskeletal system; and the sacral plexus of nerves that innervate the organs highlighted, and the soft tissues and muscles for example the buttocks and the perineum.

> *"I flow through life with ease and grace and abundance comes to me naturally."*

Linking to the element of water and the moon, it is part of the ability of the body to flow, to avoid stagnation and rigidity and supports the various organ functions of detoxification emotionally and physically. Our human bodies are 65-70% water, the Earth percentage of water is 71%, this undoubtedly is no coincidence, you could be so bold to say, it was all planned!

When we cry, our tears are the water carrying and releasing our emotions through our eyes, the organs of sight, for us to see what emotions we need to release and set ourselves free from. Yet to also understand why are we feeling this way, what is triggering this response within you? To self-reflect as water does our reflection, to seek our inner thoughts and emotions that no longer serves us purpose nor joy.

Naturally water never stops moving, flowing and in cycle from a rain drop, to a stream, to a river, to sea and the vast ocean and then through evaporation back to a rain drop, holding an imprint of all it has been in connection with.

This also can be referenced for life, our journeys; they keep moving, expanding and evolving, growing in knowledge and understanding. Our resistance to change or holding onto old thought patterns, negative experiences and belief systems blocks this vital flow and causes stagnation and later dis-ease.

Water and certain mineral absorption are key functions of the large intestines, alongside the kidneys to regulate the balance of waters and minerals within the blood, behind which the liver is constantly feeding the kidneys of blood and toxins to be expelled from the body. Any imbalance of these organs, impairs the body removal of toxins, waste products and excess hormones, which builds up the toxicity levels and poisons, overloading and suffocating the cells optimum function.

Any imbalance within the sacral chakra will be physically represented as a range of symptoms from lower back pain, irregular or painful menstruation, increasing discomfort issues of menopause, constipation and sciatica; to fertility and impotence issues and fluid balance in the body.

Its role of balance and flow when imbalance will be highlighted in symptoms of inflexibility, restricted range of movement in all joints, inflamed arthritic joints and water retention and bloating of the lower abdominal area.

"I am free from all that serves me no purpose or joy"

Emotionally, when the energy and flow is restricted we may feel stuck in life, life has lost is colour, vibrancy and joy. We do not see a way out of the situation, like a dam to water, the course of life and excitement has been blocked.

In reverse, if over active, like fast flowing rapids, this can be intense with the constant need even addictive nature to joy, pleasure, need for reassurance, sex and drugs.

Each of our organs house our various unresolved emotions. The large intestines are the final process of release of toxic products that no longer serves the body; as well as absorbing water and producing small vitamins, especially vitamin K and vitamin B.

Together with the small intestines, they are a hypersensitive transmitter-receiver of emotions, a hundred million neurons linking to the brain, hence the saying, you feel it in your gut, *your gut instinct-*

The need for security and protection, worry, stress, the feeling of being unsupported which relates back to the level of strength and foundation of the base chakra, are held within the large and small intestines, which constricts, inflames and irritates the gut, often causing mood swings and irritability if something is not quite right or has not gone according to one's plan.

The large intestine and bladder is about letting go or what no longer serves you joy, to let go of these toxic un-serving emotions, thoughts and traumatic experiences that are restricting your flow, creativity and expansion in life.

For those that suffer from bladder infections, ask yourself is there a deep emotion or element of your life or person(s) that are "pissing" you off *(sorry the politer version doesn't really grasp the emotion!)*, are there feelings you need to express? The throat chakra compliments and supports the sacral chakra through expression of our emotions; for those who like colours, the orange of the sacral and the blue of the throat are complimentary contrasting colours.

If you find it hard to express and communicate your feelings in a way that is heard and listened; there will be a blockage within the sacral energy.

Shame and guilt, the lowest frequency of emotions, the same frequency as the metal lead, lay heavy and deep within our pelvic area and organs, through trauma, experiences and old beliefs that we have been raised into. To accept the pleasure and sensuality of our sexuality may have been frowned upon and disapproved of, so we begin to cut ourselves off from this beautiful and magical part of ourselves, which can bring us joy and the sweetness of life.

There are studies to show that the initial neural pathways to become established directly after birth are within the limbic system of the brain, which directly links to the hypothalamus and the endocrine system. Within the limbic system where memories by association are recorded, be they of pleasure and joy, or negatively through pain and fear.

These initial neural pathways of experiences and associations are believed to assist the learning process as it reinforces action that are most likely to be beneficial, rather than those that make cause pain, damage and suffering. This key physical development stage is during the cycle of the sacral chakra.

Our sacral chakra and pelvis holding and supporting the organs, soft tissues, arterial and nerves, is our bowl-like well of emotion, to receive, respond and release. The intrinsic relationship with our emotions and the limbic system is how our brain develops from our environment.

The association of smells and experiences both positive and negative, create networks of neural pathways, stimulating and integrating with the endocrine system,

Through this, we recognise the power of our emotions on our

body and mind, and how our early development stages are fundamental to how our body is crudely speaking, hard wired.

Perceptions of feeling unsafe and unsupported, feeling of rejection, traumatic situations, the environment we were raised in, social acceptable programming of "acceptable" behaviour, being told for example, not to cry, "*get over it, boys don't cry*" etc.

We begin to retain our emotions on a cellular level, unresolved and stored within the subconscious mind and unconscious body, and continue to trigger responses in other experiences, as a calling to be healed, however if not conscious and aware of this, we repeat and compound the "learnt" emotional experience.

We all have these deep rooted programming that reacts as a trigger to certain situations, however, holding awareness and objectivity to self and not to be consumed by the vortex of emotion, we can start to improve our brain's plasticity and write new positive neural pathways through visualisation and meditation, to open and release the body on a cellular, physical, emotional and spiritual level.

"I am free and living the joy of life"
"I am creating the joy I wish to see in this World"
"I am Joy and I am Living Joy"

Practicing the regular flossing exercise, which often forms part of the guided mediations and visualisation journeys I host (minus the self-pleasure – you can improvise!), is a safe way to support you to move these low vibrational emotions and thought patterns through you, this is your power- conscious alchemy!

For self-pleasure in itself, may hold much stigma and shame on its own. It will support you to connect to your body, to ask yourself what you desire, to give yourself permission to receive what you desire, without shame or guilt, to recognise old patterns of thought that blocks you from receiving joy.

It may not even be from your own experiences, it may be inherited as epigenetics, emotions in our blood carried through generations. Excitingly, it releases oxytocin- the healing love potion of a hormone, freely available within you!

When practicing self-awareness, flossing or not, the key is not to get into the story of the thought of emotion, the power is recognising and acknowledging it, and holding space for you to decide whether you continue the loop of negative thought and emotion. Or do you break the pattern through conscious choice – to choose joy and to know that you are worthy of joy? For joy is your birthright and sovereignty – anything else is the illusion of fear!

A block may well be because you feel you are not worthy, for you feel guilty and ashamed for action(s) you have taken in life. This is the moment whether you decide to forgive yourself, or you continue to self-sabotage and inflict emotional pain, which overtime may well become pain and dis-ease.

A beautiful prayer that I practice on a regular basis, especially around the full moon, is the Hawaiian Ho'oponopono Prayer, as the full moon is the most aligned time to release, to let go, to forgive!

Ho'oponopono interpretation, means, to bring back life's balance, to make things right,

"I Forgive You.
Please Forgive Me
I am Sorry
I Love You
Thank You"

For me, I take it further as an intention as a prayer from my Soul and for all of my incarnations as an energetic being – for when one has acted in fear and separation.

I set the intention to send to all other Souls I have incarnated with, to finally set us all free! Free from Soul Contracts that no longer serve us. Interestingly when I do this, I can feel the relief and sense of joy of mine and the other Souls finally being released from these karmic patterns, which have been played over and over!

Can it really be that simple, when we take responsibility as a whole energetic being, without the fear of judgement and persecution, and we alchemise it, just like that!

Personally I feel it is, it is the belief that has us believe that nothing is that easy – question to this is – why not?

I invite you to note any thoughts, understandings, aha moments...

19.

SOLAR PLEXUS- MANIPURA
"The Lustrous Gem – The City of Gems"

The third and fourth chakras, the solar plexus alongside the heart chakra are the chakras for relationship, our inner and outer world. They integrate our energy with the environment and the people around us developing our personal power and space, to embody our Sovereignty – to grow as a person in our true self, to recognise the opportunities and the potential hazards and dangers, to ensure our survival, yet also to thrive.

Overview

The Solar Plexus – is our personal power, our inner masculine strength and courage, to be present and seen, to take up our space and place in this world, and to bring our dreams and creativity to fruition.

It is represented by the element of Fire, the Sun and the colour of golden yellow, providing energy, focus and self-esteem. Yellow is the colour of sunshine and it is associated with joy, happiness, intellect, and energy of life itself.

It is our emotional intelligence of our gut instinct, to hold and embody the discernment of what is pure and in alignment to our desires, our blueprint, what is ours and what is not, to absorb what we need, to learn lessons and greater wisdom.

The blessings and teachings of life, to give us the energy to thrive and create, and the innate wisdom to release what we no longer need, be that physically, emotionally and mentally.

Cycle of Nature and development – the solar plexus begins its development as a small child, starting around 18 months to about 4 years old, a stage often referred to as the terrible twos, as we begin a step of independence of our mind, wants and desires. This is when language develops alongside the understanding of time and establishing our independence and healthy boundaries.

Our gut/brain is an imperative boundary to ensure our health and wellbeing, any boundaries compromised will also affect our gut health. At this formative age, we are sponges absorbing the said and unsaid words, patterns and beliefs and the behaviours of others from our environment. At this age up to puberty, we take these on as our own, alongside the belief that what is happening in our external world is our responsibility, as the emotional, mentally and energetic boundaries have not been formed in our awareness.

Our subconscious mind is in Theta, receiving it all that becomes our beliefs and patterns, creating neural pathways of thought, affecting our central nervous state and our endocrine and hormonal health. Our gut and unconscious body becomes the library of our experiences, thoughts and senses.

To be honest, it can take a lifetime for some to understand our healthy boundaries, the first step in our health and wellbeing is recognising that there is such a thing as healthy boundaries. Especially if they were not shown to you as a child, then it is a matter of learning the unlearning, in conscious discernment and compassion for self.

A little Gem for you -Interestingly, I would also say the solar plexus stems from conception too, as it is recognised now that our mircobiome, the micro-intelligence that beholds DNA and learnt experiences of the environment, which gives life to the mitochondria and influences our personality and behaviours- comes only from the Mother. It is actually what makes us unique in diversity to our DNA, and can be traced through our feminine lineage, further than blood can!

Physical Representation– The solar plexus encompasses from the xyphoid process (the distal part of the centre of the sternum/breast bone, where bone stops and flesh begins) to the naval, on a fascia perspective from the diaphragm above the pelvic girdle and reproductive organs, enveloped in layers of peritoneum.

The solar plexus is a collection of nerves, also called the celiac plexus, a complex system of radiating nerves and ganglia, forming part of the sympathetic nervous system. It plays an important role in the functioning of the stomach, duodenum, spleen, liver, gallbladder, pancreas, small intestines, kidneys and adrenal glands. There are over hundred million nerve cells within the gut, collectively called the enteric nervous system, this system in the gut contains up to five times as many neurons as the number of neurons in the spinal cord.

This innate body intelligence has been down played and forgotten, our health is reconnecting the healthy boundaries of the gut/brain barrier to retain discernment and to sustain our inner tutor, our intuition.

Balance and optimum flow – When the Manipura Chakra/solar plexus is in balance, we are able to be within one's own counsel, body and mind, this inner warrior and belief through self-acceptance and holding an inner knowing. To have a balance of energy to achieve daily practices, finding time to rest and restore and to focus on how our energy is spent. To have the ability to energetically and emotionally cut cords and let go of negative energy, situations and thinking, to release the past and step into the present. We have a mental energy that is clear, focused and discerning, which highlights the intrinsic relationship of our gut brain and the blood/brain barrier.

Imbalance symptoms- If unbalanced the solar plexus emotionally will have the constant need and drive to be busy without focus or direction, can often be scattered, with lots of ideas yet not finding the time or focus to create. This physically is represented in a lack of energy, feeling tired quite often to chronic fatigue symptoms.

Regularly catch colds and feel unwell to disease, due to the impact of the immune system. Often seen as digestion complications and discomfort, for example, IBS, IBD bloating, hot flushes (liver), diabetes II, poor mineral absorption, food intolerances, and indigestion.

These symptoms also link into our throat chakra boundaries, as our digestion is fed by what we allow in physically, emotionally and mentally.

Musculoskeletal issues tend to be from the lower back to the shoulders and neck, hence any back issues will most likely by affected by the solar plexus and organs within.

Emotionally you may feel there is no spontaneity in life, often letting other people "walk" over you, or feel you are being taken advantage of; lacking focus, purpose and direction in life.

Or the opposite if over powering, often get angry, aggressive and over-controlling with people and situations, becoming obsessive about things.

If you relate to being an empathy/empathetic, meaning you are open and sensitive to others emotional states of being, you may well find you take on their energy, if too absorbed in their story and/or the desire to take away their pain and discomfort. Which leads to random pains, the saying "coming out in sympathy", mood swings, depression and melancholy without the understanding why? This can also be due to an open crown chakra, as we become open to the collective energy.

This distinct lack of boundaries and discernment may be why we see the Empath/Narcissist relationship, one with no boundaries and the other forcing through, exploiting the Empath's traits of absorbing others, which has them believe it is them that is the issue, through prolonged forms of manipulation such as gas-lighting.

"I am a Miracle in Itself"

Solar Plexus

The solar plexus is a fusion of many energies and functions namely our digestion, immune system and nervous system.

Nervous System -

Neurologically, the gut houses its own enteric nervous system, consisting of circa hundred million neurons, reading and evaluating our environment and other people, our feelings, thoughts, and emotions. It is our centre of knowing, our gut instinct, which in our western culture we have become detached from and focus more so on the importance to think, analyse and hold a definite knowing and credibility, seeking proof externally to us through our minds.

Our solar plexus and gut holds this inner knowing as our brains would be overloaded with these messages, it is not until action or awareness is required, does the brain become notified.

The gut and the brain have a bidirectional communication pathway. They send messages back and forth to each other all day long, via the cranial Vagus Nerve X. This nerve extends from the hypothalamus and brain stem, to the gut and connects our central nervous system with our enteric nervous system of the gastrointestinal tract.

The vagus nerve forms the large majority of the parasympathetic nervous system, our rest digest, feed breed state of being, it is the M1 of motorways, or Route 20, the health of this nerve is intrinsic to our health and wellbeing, mind and body.

In addition to this, if this wasn't enough, the gut has the responsibility of producing about 75% of the brain's neurotransmitters which are responsible for cellular communication, one of such is Serotonin. our gut and solar plexus is our beacon, transmitter and receiver of information and thoughts.

This communication of the gut brain to the brain seeks a balance and flow. However, when it becomes overwhelmed and restricted through over thinking, worrying stress, trauma, fears, unresolved emotions, the brain's coping mechanism is to download/ or unload into the organs, especially within the digestion system, causing constriction on a cellular level overtime.

As 80% of the vagus neural pathway is communication from the organs that it innervates to the brain, you can see how also the health of the gut will be transferred to the brain.

Therefore, any inflammation within the gut, from toxins, chemicals, intolerant food types and surgery, will inflame and impinge the function of the vagus nerve. Causing symptoms such as stress, anxiety, mood swings and depression, brain fog, and if the blood brain barrier is compromised – more degenerative diseases such as Alzheimer's (type III diabetes), Parkinson's.

Herbicides actually breakdown the natural methylation cycle the Shikimate Pathway, which is fundamental for essential amino acids, which are building blocks for intrinsic neuroendocrines, namely Serotonin, Melatonin, Dopamine.

There are nine essential amino acids, which mean they cannot be synthesized by human or other mammalian cells, thus they must be supplied from external source in our diet. The nine includes histidine, isoleucine, leucine, lysine, methionine, *phenylalanine, threonine, tryptophan,* and valine, which are proven to be directly and indirectly affected by glyphosate (weed killer).

Digestion and Immune System-
Connecting to your Inner Knowing — Your Inner-Tuition and Teacher

The solar plexus incorporates our digestion system, breaking down the food with our teeth, from the saliva of our mouths to the acid of the stomach; the churn of bile from the liver and gallbladder and pancreatic juices, to form what is called the chime; to then be broken down further by the small intestines, for the vitamins and minerals to be absorbed, providing vital proteins and energy for our cells to function.

Our digestion system supports 70-80% of our immune system, home to white blood cells that are constantly reading, evaluating viruses, bacteria and fungi within our blood and system. It stores and categorises information similar to a library of everything the body encounters.

The digestion system is like an intense training camp for the white blood cells; when immature cells are formed, they need to go through a rigorous training programme establishing what is a healthy cell and what is not, recognising when to act and when not to.

The intestines have layers of membranes and villi, little fingers that absorb the nutrients and support peristalsis. These, in a healthy balanced gut, are coated and protected by various strains of bacteria, viruses and fungi, and a mucus membrane, supporting the immune cells in their training and removing those, that prove to be rogue and start attacking healthy cells.

Health issues occur when there is an imbalance and fatigue within the gut membrane. Through stressful busy lifestyles, trauma, drugs, antibiotics, processed foods, chemicals in our food, home and care products, herbicides, such as glyphosate and the toxicity of the air that we breathe.

All of which, breakdown this healthy gut flora that is protecting our digestion and immune system, causing the blood-brain barrier, the membranes and the villi to erode and weaken, severely impacting the many functions of the digestion, immune and nervous system.

Also, from becoming too much of a germ-phobic sterile culture, it has affected the efficiency of the mucus membrane, as the bacteria is actually needed in balance to protect the membrane, as well as being protected from.

The ability to absorb the vital nutrients via the villi for the body to operate is reduced, you may find you are eating the right foods, yet it isn't a matter of lacking, it is a matter of the body being unable to absorb and retain.

The barrier membranes are weakened, often referred to as a "leaky gut", or I see it as a hose pipe with many holes along it depending on the severity, or a tea bag mesh that has opened and become too baggy, you get the picture! This then allows chaos to reign, the immature white blood cells that have not finished their extensive training programme, go rogue vandalising and attacking healthy cells, known as autoimmune diseases.

Undigested food particles go into the blood stream, impacting and overloading the liver and the kidneys to increase their detoxification process, becoming more fatigued and inflamed as they are overworked and without the nutrients they need to function, which have further implications to the organs' health and their multiple functions.

The blood-brain membrane through the bidirectional communication pathway between the gut and the brain weakens, especially through chemicals, in our food, drugs and our environment. This breakdown allows toxins to penetrate the Central Nervous System, with many studies highlighting the connection to Alzheimer's, autism and cancer.

Therefore, we can see how the beautiful melody that would

normally be this orchestra of organs creating peaceful, flowing harmony and homeostasis, becomes rather like a Dick Van Dyke's attempt in the original Mary Poppins- chaotic, unpleasant and painful, for those that are not old enough to remember, see the link below for a little entertainment.

https://www.youtube.com/watch?v=B_rVzBt20N0

The health of our gastrointestinal system is vital for our health and wellbeing. Any imbalance will affect our immune system, energy levels and metabolic functions, mental health, endocrine system and musculoskeletal; from the lumbar vertebrae to the neck and shoulders, due to the nerve and arterial supply travelling through the spinal cord to the organs.

Quite often, lower lumbar back and groin pain is due to the restriction of the mesentery root (similar to a stem of lettuce), which connects directly to the spine and feeds the nerves and blood to the intestines. It also will be the reverse, any spinal or vertebra restrictions and injuries, would affect these key supplies to the intestines affecting their function.

The large intestine is where we store worry, especially about our loved ones, being over protective and/or feeling out of control of the situation, especially as our children grow, as we are unable to protect them as much as we wish to at times.

I have had clients come with excruciating lower back pain, constipation and family stress as symptoms, they all relate to one another. The key healing was the ability to breathe, surrender and trust, that can only come from an open heart, not the mind - thus enabling the central nervous system to calm and switch to the parasympathetic to heal, as well as the amazing alchemy that I bring to the sessions of course!

"I am Amazing"

The Elemental and Emotional

The Solar plexus is represented with the element of fire, providing warmth, comfort and nourishment for growth. However, fire also brings fear and terror when out of control, which is echoed in the emotional aspect of the solar plexus.

Fear is a fundamental emotion which triggers a catalogue of other emotions and reactions in our daily lives. Fear arises in any situation where the thought or outcome seems beyond the capacity of the mind to determine. The mind and body being unable to relax, rest and rejuvenate, and conjures up limiting scenarios and obstacles, becoming locked in a self-defeating, not good enough belief system, causing a continuous stress on a cellular level.

Remember FEAR —Fears are Emotions that Aren't Real

The solar plexus cycle of nature begins to mature and develop within us when we are 18 months to 4 years old, when language and expressions evolves, alongside the understanding of passing of time and beginning to acknowledge ourselves and emotions. It is often labelled as the terrible twos, as this is when we are learning who we are, growing and establishing our personal power and voice.

Finding the balance of boundaries and discipline as a guardian is fundamental, as the lack of constructive discipline and boundaries creates an overpowering egotistical child. Whilst in reverse, too much discipline will stop a sense of autonomy and creates a base of fear and suppression of the child's expression and creativity.

As a child, our relationship with adults and authority figures, such as school teachers, shapes how we evolve and grow. Often emotions of fear, shame and guilt are harboured and imprinted within us, held heavy within the solar plexus, the sacral chakra and the organs within.

This may forge patterns of allowing others to overpower and control even throughout adulthood, over giving to others, the people pleaser. You feel you are unable to form healthy boundaries, for the fear that lays within our subconscious mind and unconscious body. The fear of rejection and abandonment certainly plays a role in our behaviour – highlighting the relationship of the solar plexus and limbic system, our emotion control centre including the sacral chakra.

You may be creative and have lots of ideas, however, unable to focus and channel one's energy to manifesting these ideas, quite possibly creating big ideas, yet become overwhelmed by the prospect of how to achieve. This forms illusions of obstacles driven by fear that one is not enough, scattering your energy and thoughts too thinly.

In reverse, a dominant and strict upbringing can equally manifest issues with authority and rules. The trigger of feeling controlled, becomes an over controlling of others and situations, ignoring wisdom, guidance and advice from others, often seeing flashes of anger, ignited by certain people or situations.

Freedom, is definitely a question we are asking ourselves subconsciously here, Am I Free? However, interestingly, the paradox is that we need boundaries to have Freedom – one cannot exist without the other – just like the gut membrane and the microbiome, the key is finding the balance which comes from conscious discernment.

Over authoritative and strict upbringings may also lead us to believe that we as in ourselves are not enough. Forging patterns and belief systems that we constantly need to achieve to prove our self-worth, that this recognition and attainment of worthiness can only be claimed externally to us, driving this self-perpetuating cycle of un-fulfillment and stress, that is detrimental to our health and wellbeing.

The Alchemy and Power of Anger

Held predominantly in the liver - anger in our society is often seen as a negative, if female, it is said it must be the hormones *(as a female I need to add in a ggrrh here!)*. For men it is seen as more an "acceptable" emotion for a male to show, as all others are perceived to be an act of weakness, the rejection of the feminine side of us all, male or female.

However, anger is the tip of the emotional iceberg, what we see on the surface is anger, yet underneath in the waters of emotion, are shame, guilt, hurt and fears. Therefore, anger is not a negative when we become consciously aware of the trigger within, to actively seek the root of this emotional response and the path, to heal old wounds and release of old fears, beliefs and thought patterns.

Through my own self-healing and with others, I actually see the huge benefit of channelling one's inner anger and rage consciously, as it opens the heart and liver to move and alchemise, what has ultimately become a smoldering furnace, creating suffocation and inflammation in our body and mind.

When we connect to this deep hurt and betrayal, we recognise the love and self-worth that is actually underneath and fuelling it to move through us with an open compassionate conscious heart, to be acknowledged and remembered.

It is actually the voice that is saying *"I deserve better, I am worthy of so much more, I am worthy of love!"* – Unless we allow ourselves to hear this voice through the process of conscious rage healing, we will never remember our worth and the unconditional love that is already within us! And our bodies continue to be inflamed and thus ill health and disease.

The liver and the heart are the alchemists of the anger and rage, however, I also do feel and see it stored within our breasts, womb, yoni, and bladder as women. As you recognise the trauma that women have endured for millennia, which as we know now, can carry through our epigenetics –I do believe we are here to be the pattern breakers by acknowledging and healing in our bodies.

As a mirror, I actually see this unconscious trauma in men, carried through the microbiome/feminine lineage, held within the sacral energy and groin, yet more as shame, to feel ashamed of one's masculinity, which may be due to the blood line of abused women in his lineage, as an unconscious belief. This is what I would say is the shadow of the new termed *Toxic Masculinity*, as it is blocking men to step up fully and proudly within their true masculine energy, which is to protect and discern, a strength and power to be used wisely, and not for control or abuse of this power upon others!

I do feel society has become muddied, women heavily in their masculine as this is what has been needed to be seen, heard, to be equal and to survive. Yet along the way, we have forgotten our grace, our femininity, to be supported by the masculine.

We need to heal both sides, the masculine, the feminine, the male the female, to find this healthy equilibrium, to feel safe, to be held, to allow the space for the masculine to step up in a way that is pure and serving that holds the feminine. To enable the power of the feminine to return, as she is the protector and healer of the heart – she is the alchemist should she choose to be! This is where society can heal, as we forgive, yet never forget – so we never return to what it was before!

"I am Enough"

Up until 2020 came about, being busy was the "in" thing, time was always an excuse not to do things. The pandemic for some, was an awakening, a gratitude of life and our Earth, our relationships and our health, which inspired many to make changes. However, with the "cost of living", this way of being has certainly crept back in, as the media and powers to be, play the strings of scarcity. Depending whether we are more conscious of, will determine if and how we change!

When we find time for ourselves, jumping off this crazy conveyor belt set on hyper speed, to know that simply being you is enough, we start to hold space for our thoughts. We ground, connect to Mother Nature, enjoy the beauty that is around us, the sounds of the birds and insects. We open ourselves to joy, contentment and fulfillment and a more peaceful existence.

Our solar plexus, is not only a library of immunity recording, it is also our library of thoughts, recorded and imprinted within the organs themselves through the neural pathways. Holding our beliefs and thought processes, we become what we think, positive or negative. We are a beacon, receiving and transmitting a frequency of our thoughts.

Imagine our thoughts and emotions are musical notes, what tune or song would you be emanating, is it uplifting, open, expansive joyful, is it a lower deeper darker tune, is it slow monotone or is techno music raving creating chaos and buzzing?

Take a moment, listen and hold awareness of your frequency and the music you are creating through thoughts and being.

As energy attracts energy, be aware of your frequency, your vibration of thoughts, beliefs and emotions. Freeing ourselves from all the restrictive fearful thought patterns and beliefs, we change the pattern, the neurological pathways of mind, heart and body.

Say to yourself every morning when you begin to wake up, before the to-do lists float within your conscious mind,

Be the thoughts that you wish to be and create.

"I AM ENOUGH, I AM ENOUGH, I AM ENOUGH, just the way I am!"

"My light, love, uniqueness and presence in this world, is a gift."

"I stand in the light of my uniqueness with acceptance"

"I am a beautiful spectrum of light"

"My presence in this World is a gift"

"As I take on new challenges, I feel calm, confident, and powerful."

"I feel motivated to pursue my purpose."

"I am ambitious and capable."

"I forgive myself for past mistakes, and I learn from them."

"The only thing I need to control is how I respond to situations."

"I have the courage to create positive change in my life."

"I stand in my personal power."

"I release myself from all fears that no longer serve me joy of purpose"

I invite you to note any thoughts, understandings, aha moments...

20.

THE HEART CHAKRA- ANAHATA
"My Heart is my Anchor, My Love is my Strength"

Overview

Heart Chakra – Anahata in Sanskrit means "unstuck" "unhurt". Tt is represented by the element of Air and the colour of green and/or pink. The heart is about maintaining balance in all aspects of ourselves, our physical, emotional, mental and spiritual bodies. The heart chakra governs unconditional love, and our relationship with ourselves internally and those externally to us.

The mantra used to open the energy of the chakra is YAM

Cycle of Nature and development – our heart chakra develops over the period of 4-7 years old and represents our relationships outside the immediate family. The energy centre relates to our self-esteem and self-acceptance and our ability to give and receive in balance.

If love and relationships have always been conditional, manipulation, emotional price tags, for example, *"you would do this if you love me, I will love you if you do this, make me proud!"* Underlying feelings of guilt and grief are caused by not receiving enough love, unconditional love, by simply being you is not enough, creates difficulties and unhealthy attachments through life, if not realised or addressed.

Conditional Love and Kindness - Is not Love or Kindness
It is Manipulation!

Physical -the heart chakra is located near the centre of the breastbone or sternum and is associated with the thoracic vertebrae area and ribs, extending and including the arms. The physical organs are the heart, lungs and upper respiratory system, namely the trachea, larynx and pharynx, nose.

The endocrine gland is the Thymus, situated above the heart that is vital for our growth and support of the immune system, especially in childhood.

The sympathetic nerve plexuses represented, are the cardiac and pulmonary feeding the heart and lungs. The cardiac plexus sits superiorly to the pulmonary plexus, also connecting the oesophageal plexus. The Vagus nerve (CNX), branches out to these plexuses, enabling homeostasis and health.

The physical organs and areas of the body represented and linked by this chakra are characterised by their actions of expansion and contraction, opening and closing, drawing inwards and pushing outwards.

Balance and optimum flow –the heart chakra throughout all its elements is about being in balance and flow. The balance of the lungs oxygen and CO_2; the balance of self-discipline, self-acceptance and freedom; the balance within relationships of autonomy and sharing, that have no ties allowing unconditional love to flow; the balance of letting go to receive; the balance of the inner and outer worlds, our personal needs and the needs of others to the highest good for all. To expand and grow in power whilst keeping harmony with the Earth and everything around us

Imbalance symptoms- when this balance and flow is restricted, it is seen physically in a shortened posture, a closing within and around the heart chakra, causing pain and restrictions in the mid thoracic area, under the nipple line to the xyphiod process to the neck, shoulders and extending to the arms; and breathing difficulties from asthma to COPD.

Without self-love and self-acceptance, there is stress and dis-ease emotionally and physically. Personally I believe all pain, discomfort and illnesses of mind and body relates to the open flow and balance of love for ourselves and our relationships to the external world!

Blood issues high and low blood pressure; circulation complications e.g. Raynaud's disease, which also links to tension within the sacral chakra (emotions and heart expression); poor nourishment and absorbency issues e.g. tiredness to chronic fatigue, skin hair and nails; inflammation and immune system issues e.g. arthritis, autoimmune diseases, in fact all illnesses are inflammation of the body to a cellular level.

Emotionally, one forms attachment to external things, experiences and relationships that are un-serving of neither joy nor happiness. Unable to let go and forgive others and sometimes oneself, holding shame, guilt hurt, anger building walls around the heart disconnecting to self and others, often being cold, cynical and judgemental of oneself and others.

Alternatively, too open, pouring ones heart to others to receive love being a "people pleaser" to the detriment of oneself, unhealthy boundaries, where others take advantage; being over the top emotionally and the feeling of jealousy.

Finding the Balance through Coherence of Heart, Mind & Body

"My heart is open to the flow of love and life"

Anahata in Sanskrit means to be "*unstruck, unhurt*", which gives this beautiful idea and image that our heart can never really be broken, that it is a balance of giving and receiving for our hearts to truly awaken.

The art of balance is the theme that runs through all levels of the heart chakra, represented by the element of air. Air flows from areas of high pressure to low pressure, always seeking the equilibrium. Likewise, the heart chakra is constantly seeking the balance between external stimuli and internal emotions. Without this equilibrium we would not be able to adapt to situations, to evolve grow and expand in life.

From my own personal experiences and with clients, our health and happiness comes back to how much self-love and self-acceptance we hold for in our hearts. When you love and accept yourself, knowing that you are enough, just by simply being you, that you are already achieving as you are, a Miracle in itself, you open your heart to flow in unconditional love, this infinite and abundant flow of giving and receiving.

I have had the privilege to hold space and witness many clients shift pain, both physically and emotionally, when they have connected to the love within them, it is pure and beautiful!

"I am A Miracle in Itself"

Holding deep within a cellular level, allowing the words "I am Enough" to resonate to your core, you take the foot off the accelerator in life and switch to cruise mode, knowing that you are good enough, just the way you are. With no need to prove your worth, that you ARE worthy and that life is not about constant achievements and gains at full pelt. In reality life is about happiness, joy, fulfillment and purpose, which then flows naturally to you in abundance.

You sit back more comfortably and start to enjoy the ride, the journey of life, you see the beauty of the landscape of your journey, and you feel free, liberated, excited about what opportunities and experiences there is to come in life.

"I am free from all that serves me no purpose or joy"
"I am free"

It is widely recognised that we inherit our physical appearance and genes from our parents; however, it isn't as well known that we also inherit thought patterns and belief systems from our ancestor and guardians.

These old beliefs and ways of thought, are passed through generations, the *"should, have, need to"* aspects of life that mould and form us into our "social acceptable" ways of being, the social etiquette and expectations. Sometimes these rules are required to live in harmony with each other, however, these rules and ways are often controlling and do not serve us joy or purpose.

Examples of such beliefs can be; to not question authority,

simply accept the rules and infrastructure, even if they do not make sense; accepting the belief that individuals of authority have a power over you. How often do we hear our children say "but Why?, which sometimes does not have an answer apart from "it just is!", I believe our children are here to remind us to question the rules and beliefs and not to simple accept them as they are.

If you were brought up in a family that struggled financially, that you believe that you have to work so hard to achieve, that life is about working hard, possibly feeling unsupported financially. Subconsciously always having the worry of having enough money, or even that money is not something you deserve or worthy of, or does not happen easily for you. That people with money are better than those that do not; somehow they are achieving more; that money is about achievement and proving oneself to the world; to be accepted by others our family, friends and society.

To not to follow your dreams as they will not support you, that dreams are just dreams not reality! This forms your subconscious relationship with the energy and the flow of money and abundance,

The dynamics of our parents/guardian relationships imprints onto us, we often adopt the same dynamic in our relationships. The unsaid roles each individual plays, what is acceptable and unacceptable behaviour, how healthy were those boundaries, how much love and joy was in the relationship. Was it a matter of supporting each other's happiness or was there an imbalance of control?

Being raised by a single parent, the degree of hardship or joy, the feeling of abandonment of support, possibly developing the thought process that you have to support yourself, and that others cannot be trusted, being unwilling to ask for help, becoming guarded of the heart?

"I am free to be the light I am here to be"

As our heart chakra matures, we become aware and start to examine these old beliefs and thought processes, whether they are valid or serving to us, especially in times of minimal joy or purpose, when we feel repressed and restricted.

Quite often, outright rebellion seems the only option to break free of the suffocating patterns, although society does not tend to appreciate such movements of freedom. Whatever the rules and regulations of society, outright rebellion is criticised and has become primary targets by the media, our today's behaviour of censorship, who tend to take the tribal stance of the establishment. Rejecting new concepts and unique insights, often derogatively labelled as conspiracy theorists, using our primitive psychology that fears social rejection to control.

If society held a more open communication, that allows all perspectives with compassion and no judgement, without the fear of "insulting" someone, we would have more trust. We would grow in humility, society would take responsibility of ill-doing, it would foster an environment of conscious behaviour, we would allow ourselves to feel what is right in our heart from all the senses, not just being told what to think!

With Artificial Intelligence increasing into our lives, when it is unknown what is true and what is not, we will become more and more reliant to listen to our hearts and gut. Our inner wisdom and feeling rather, than our mental input and sensory!- I believe this is another "cosmic coaching" to encourage us to move to the intelligence and innate wisdom that is held within our hearts.

"My heart is free and healed from all the wounds of the past"

When we hold in our hearts self-love and self-acceptance, we can be free from these chains of restraints, the fear of not being good enough, the fear of being rejected from the tribe, our primal survival emotions.

We are strong within, we have the fire in our belly and the light of love in our hearts, we do not seek neither praise nor approval from others, or fear of judgement from our tribe or society. Through this evolution to our hearts, we become aware of the chains, restraints and restrictions, growing beyond the need of them, which before were our illusion of security.

Breaking free from the attachments of old belief systems, thought processes and fears that restrict your true unique light of greatness.

The old beliefs which tell a story that everything you need is externally to you, that it is a matter of a constant search outside of yourself, the beliefs that you need to be a certain way to achieve in life, that you are not worthy or deserving of love, joy, health and wealth in abundance.

These belief and thought processes overtime cause a constant level of stress of the mind and body, which overtime is what constricts our cells, reducing the flow of nutrients and nourishment, changes our gene expression, causing dis-ease.

However, our truth is the opposite to this ancestral un-serving belief system that in passed through generations of society. What we need, is already within us, the love, the joy, the wisdom, it is learning to trust this, and learn the unlearning!

"Everything I need is Already within me"

The heart is the epicentre of our mind and body, it is the combining force that connects and supports the body as one. It is the centre and unites the physical, emotional, mental and spiritual bodies.

The heart has a frequency so expansive, which is 5000 times greater than the brain. The arteries and capillaries expand and reach out to each cell, feeding with nutrients and oxygen, the vital elements of health and vitality. Without such, the cells would die, constrict within themselves causing dysfunction and disease.

The heart connects to all of our body, to each artery and capillary, and there is a nerve connecting to either or both of our central nervous systems, our brain and the enteric nervous system, within the gastrointestinal system which works independently to the mind. The heart through these intricate connections and balance, communicates as one, the heart holds a knowing within.

With the deep connection of the heart and the gut brain, the body feels, absorbs and processes emotions, our relationships, the environment and the energetic field around them. Together they form this intricate, essential and beautiful relationship of an inner knowing, that is imperative for our survival, our happiness, our health and joy.

To be able to understand what is serving you joy and what is not, to know when something feels right, to get an odd heavy feeling in your stomach and heart like a pull to say, *"this path isn't right for me!"*,

Or in balance, your heart expands within your chest filled with joy and excitement, butterflies in your stomach when you meet someone you like, your heart races in expansion, you cannot help but smile. These are the beautiful instinctive reactions our bodies are telling us, for us to listen and observe and to trust ourselves, our inner knowing.

Quite often we feel these sensations, yet our mind wades in and overrules, dampening our connection and response to these vital feeling centres, this inner wisdom, our inner teacher, our inner-tuition ultimately with fear underlying this reaction.

To understand and become aware of our thoughts and actions, and why we think and act the way we do, if it is not of love, kindness and compassion, then it is of fear, deep within the layers of emotions. How often do we hear the saying, the head overruling the heart, how fear overrules our opportunities of joy and love in our lives?

The key is the balance of heart and mind coherence, the heart leading and the mind and central nervous system trusting it, so it is calm and moving with you, rather than against you. The more you practice connecting to your body through an open heart, the more you will become to understand your true *"yes"* and aligned answer, and what doesn't align to you, from a visceral reaction and sensation.

"I serve in a way that serves my joy and contentment"

I shall let you into a secret, well it is not really a secret, it is something many of us have denied- our purpose in life, which is to be happy and to support each other's happiness through love, kindness and compassion. In Buddhism, the Dharma is the Path of Happiness,

When we appreciate, recognise and connect to these deep inner knowing and wisdom centres, we form a beautiful listening and communication system in balance with our mind, heart, gut brain and body. We hold a space of calm, as there is a peace from this inner-knowing.

You are not constantly searching externally to yourself, placing the value purely on the need to know through our minds, to have external confirmation, this illusion of control, which can often cause so much conflict within. Instead, you create and hold a peaceful, joyful sanctuary within your body through self-love and self-acceptance, reducing the internalised stress that is so detrimental to our health and wellbeing, mind and body.

It is so imperative to carve out time for you every day to hold space for your mind and body, through breath, awareness and meditation. To ground and be within and centred, to quieten the spin that overwhelms us, as it is constantly fuelled through stress, a sense of feeling out-of-control. This perpetual motion of cause and effect, becomes a perception of confirmation of one's thoughts and fears.

Holding an objective view of oneself and our environment and others, allows us to step out of the emotional vortex that can so easily whip us off our feet and carry us into the storm. This attention and awareness permits us to see our un-serving triggers, thoughts, beliefs and emotions, to then be empowered with the intent to be free of all that serves no purpose or joy.

"My Heart is my Anchor, My Love is my Strength"

Our Physical & Emotional Relationship to our Heart
"I am Love and I am Loved"

The heart is the control centre of our blood serving every cell in the body with vital nutrients. Blood is represented through the emotion of love, how much love we feel within for ourselves, how well do we nourish ourselves with self-love?

If you have issues that relate to poor nourishment and absorption of minerals and vitamins, such as fatigue, fibromyalgia, poor skin, hair and nails, diabetes II, digestion issues, they all follow a trail and the unpeeling of layers to how much love and kindness we hold for ourselves.

These health conditions directly relate to poor nourishment, mineral and vitamin absorption, yet deeper, the vital proteins and amino acids are not available for cell repair and growth and our immune system is affected as 70-80% is within the gastrointestinal system, causing inflammation.

Inflammation is the fundamental cause of all disease, anything with "itis" in its name is inflammation. It is a broad statement I know, however, for me, my experiences and with clients, dis-ease is the matter of the heart, of self-love and how much love we hold for ourselves,

To feel worthy and deserving of love, for love to be unconditional, to hold self-acceptance of your uniqueness, that you are loveable just the way you are, that you are enough by simply being you.

It is vital for our health and wellbeing to find the balance of love, to be able to give and receive in perfect balance, forming a beautiful healthy boundary that is only permeable to love. So often we are giving out so much love and kindness to others, yet not giving to ourselves.

Overtime, one becomes drained, desponded, and resentful, as you feel you are giving away so much of yourself, yet not receiving in return. Quite often this raises feelings of hurt and anger (anger being the cocktail of all emotions), escalating the un-serving belief that one is not worthy of love, which escalates and is compounded by events, which is reflected as confirmation of these old beliefs.

I would even extend symptoms to breast cancer, as we are truly in the heart centre here. Breasts are beautiful, and are for our pleasure as women as we choose, they are there to nurture and forge life with deep connection and love to an infant as we breastfeed. When bottle feeding, we hold our babies close to our hearts as we feed and nurture them, for our babies survival yet also to thrive, to feel love, safety and connection.

Our breasts are a symbol of love and life, to give and receive, if we are carrying patterning that blocks us from receiving love unconditionally, and/or becoming a sponge to negativity. Possibly from others, be that through toxic relationships; abuse; lack of self-worth; and carrying guilt and shame. In doing so, we restrict this key energetic flow, to receive love and oxygen to our cells.

It can bring up our relationship with our Mother, for men the heart chakra certainly holds the Mother wounds. Our mother from her own subconscious and unconscious wounding may have been distant and emotionally detached, heavily in the shadows of masculine behaviour, busy and not fully present, to abandonment, abuse, alcoholism.

In my 1:1 sessions, Mother Mary often works through me, as I connect the heart and mind together in a supportive hold, often with the client's hands on mine. For them to hold and receive, the most beautiful unconditional love pours through and into the person's heart, healing these wounds that bring a sense of inner peace, a quietening of mind, a resolution and place of acceptance.

To me, this transformation is a process of emotional-energetic alchemy, it is not about re-traumatising the person, it is about alchemy of the pain, anger, hurt and grief back to love – our inner gold!

Healing our Mother wounds enables us to have healthier relationships, first with ourselves and then flowing to others.

I invite you to say these affirmations out loud with your hands on your heart chakra, listen and observe in how comfortable it feels, what thoughts come to mind as you do:

"I choose Love"
"I am Worthy of Love"
"I am Love"
"I Love Myself"
"I love every bump and curve of my body"
"I am a Miracle"
"I fully accept and love myself"
"I Am Enough"
"My heart is open to the alchemy of love"

How did that feel, did those words resonate and feel true within you?

If you are anything like me a few years ago, before I came upon the journey of self-love, I felt very uncomfortable with these words, I even felt myself squirm away from them, shrinking my heart inwards and my shoulders forward, which interestingly, is a posture that is adapted with a tight heart chakra plexus.

If these did not resonate with you, it somehow felt untruthful speaking the words, please, please, please do not use this as an excuse to give yourself a hard time, this is normal! Many of us are on a journey of self-love and self-acceptance, to be able to truly recognise the uniqueness and beauty within us.

It is not surprising that we are challenged to hold this unconditional love for ourselves, the old un-serving belief systems that loving oneself is seen as egotistical, that it is a negative.

The way and the environment we were raised in. Maybe you were the elder child or had many siblings, so the narrative was to always think about others and not put yourself first, as this was seen as selfish. Again, there is always a balance of self-love, expression and consideration to others, yet not to the detriment of oneself. The healthy balanced boundaries are so vital for our health and wellness.

The heart chakra develops within us from 4 to 7 years of age and is characterised by the relationships outside the immediate family. If love and relationships were always seen as being conditional, i.e. there is an emotional price tag attached to the exchange of love, underlying feelings of guilt and grief lay seeded within causing great difficulties in exchanging, giving and receiving love through life.

Experiences of traumas and abuse compounds this negative narrative, that one is not worthy of love, that there is something wrong with you, holding guilt and shame blocking the abundant flow of love to oneself.

Quite often our parents intentionally or unintentionally label us, one is given the label of *"the Clever one" "the Creative one" "the Different one" "the Awkward/Stubborn one"*, *"the Pretty one", "the Funny one" "the Sensible one",* the labels are extensive!

These in our early years can define us, if we allow them to, it can make us believe we are only that one label and that we lack the other qualities.

This becomes an un-serving belief system that we feel is our path and blocks us being a spectrum and balance of all. It can create resentment and division between siblings, constantly comparing oneself to them and others, creating emotional reactions and feelings of jealousy and envy of their external achievements.

These labels can also be delivered and spoken in a negative tone *"your just like your Dad or Mum"* or whoever the other person feels negative towards, sowing a seed and a perception that a part of you is not good enough, there is something unworthy, or bad within you, creating the low vibrational emotions of shame and guilt.

"My Words are Magic, I speak them Magically"

If you whole heartedly accepted those words and affirmations above into every being of your body and cells, and they sang from your heart, I humbly salute you.

This is truly amazing and wonderful, as this is still a journey for me, even with my knowledge and experiences so far. Some days I'm riding on the joy wave of self-love, other days, pfff-nah, which is why paying attention to your own narrative is so important.

We can either be surfing the wave of love, joy and abundance, or down the whirlpool of self-attack, self- sabotage, it is our choice, to choose our internal words to ourselves and the external words we speak as confirmation to others.

First we need to recognise these belief systems as bull-shit, then we become the curious observer, rather than the believer, and begin to break the pattern and through conscious choices we create neural pathways to move away from the old un-serving ones.

"I am an abundant source and vessel of unconditional love"

Learning the art and power to receive, is life-changing, to be able to "take" a compliment is a wonderful exchange between two individuals. How often do we either give or are offered a compliment and it is rejected, the initial intent to be a loving exchange becomes an uncomfortable situation of subtle rejection, of both the giver and the expected receiver.

We often feel we are not worthy to accept love, due to old beliefs and thought processes, that have formed within us as we have developed in life's experiences.

To help you to receive compliments, the first person you should try it with is yourself. Go to the mirror (*I can hear some of you moaning, ah I don't like this, not this nonsense, possibly feeling uneasy!*), go for it and look at those eyes of the miracle before you... You!

Say something nice, it can simply be *"I love your toes"*, to, *"you look amazing!"*. Or if you find this hard to accept and it doesn't resonate with you, place the words *"I am willing to"* in the affirmations. *"I am willing to Love Myself"*.

This way you are saying I'm willing to get to that point in my life where I whole heartedly believe in these words, I am starting this journey of self-love and acceptance. For me, I chose the precursor of "I am willing" first, now I accept the words of self-love, most of the time, like I said it is a journey!

The Balance and Flow of Love and Life – Blood and Breath
The Breath of Life

Our lungs and the upper respiratory system are part of the heart chakra; hence any physical issues are related to the heart.

Our blood carries oxygen and carbon dioxide to each cell. Between the heart and lungs the deoxygenated blood goes through the pulmonary loop, exiting the right ventricle of the heart, through the pulmonary trunk and splitting into the right and left pulmonary arteries, transporting the deoxygenated blood to arterioles and capillary beds in the lungs.

Here, carbon dioxide is released and oxygen is absorbed. Oxygenated blood then passes from the capillary beds through venules into the pulmonary veins which transport the blood and oxygen to the left atrium of the heart, to continue this cycle and balance of nourishment and sustenance of life.

Carbon dioxide regulates the pH balance of our bodies. Regulating this intrinsic homeostasis through breath, receiving and releasing is vital in the balance of our health and wellness. If our bodies become too acidic, disease forms, when our bodies are of alkalosis, breathing respiratory issues, namely COPD, asthma, anxiety, panic attacks occur.

As mentioned in the breathing chapters, due to stress, trauma emotionally and physically, we hold in our vulnerable aspect of ourselves, the gut, thus when we breathe, the diaphragm is restricted.

Overtime this fatigues and shortens the muscle similar to an upright foetal position depending on the severity, which is seen as a primitive stance of protection of our vulnerability.

This affects how we look out into the world, eyes down or seeking the horizon – our future. This chronic position, causes tension in the occiput, the back of the head resulting in headaches and a reduce flow to the brain.

As the body always seeks balance and homeostasis, it compensates and adjusts, as the brain weighs 2.8 pounds, this imbalance affects the whole musculoskeletal system and the organs within, impinging circulation of oxygen, blood and the lymphatic flow and the function of each organ.

Forming a healthy relationship with the outside world.

The heart chakra is all about the balance of our internal world in relation to the external world and our environment.

There are more viruses and bacteria in our water, rain, oceans, rivers and seas; in our soil and in the air, than there are stars in the universe! So how do we remain healthy if we are under constant threat?

The innate immune system that lays within the upper respiratory tract, there are mucus membranes which line and protect the nasal cavity, throat, larynx, thorax and lungs that are constantly receiving data input of the external stimuli of pathogens, bacteria, fungi and viruses.

Some bacteria and viruses are of no risk and are actually required to improve our immunity, similar to a bacterial and viral upgrade of our systems, keeping in balance with Mother Earth, of which we are a creation of, that nourishes and sustains us here.

To enable this balance, the body is constantly in communication with its outside environment, knowing when to react and when not to, otherwise our body would be constantly inflamed due to our immune system fighting perceived pathogens of danger.

The thymus gland that sits snuggly behind the sternum/breast bone is an intrinsic part of our immune system producing T-cells, the white blood cells that fight the invasion of the external pathogens, which may be detrimental to our health through disease. Following the response of our immune system, the body then becomes a library of responses, storing the key codes to dissemble viruses and bacteria should we be in contact with it again.

Our gut is lined with the same epithelial mucous surface cells found in the lungs, which are protected by friendly "good" bacteria. The gut flora forming a protective barrier of the gut brain, supporting the elimination of the pathogens and imperatively it forms the blood/brain barrier, blocking these pathogens from entering our central nervous system and brain.

Any breaks, weakness of this gut lining through antibiotics, chemicals and stress, often labelled as leaky gut, allows these keys T-cells and immunity coding to be lost. The thymus gradually shrinks away as we get older and by the age of circa 65 years, no T-cells are produced, relying on the immunity storage of T-cells in our gut.

Auto-immune illnesses and inflammation are the cause of all diseases, from the names with "itis" to cancer. Therefore, I believe all illnesses come back to and are the matter of the heart, our emotional centre of love. How much love we hold for ourselves, our feelings of worthiness that nurtures and warms our heart to open and flourish in a balance of giving and receiving within the healthy boundaries of our internal and external worlds.

It is in our blood!

Due to the emotional connection, the heart chakra links and supports the sacral chakra the centre and well of emotion, which is represented by the element of water. Interestingly the blood plasma is made up of circa 92% water and 8% blood, so we can see how our blood reflects, carries and embodies our emotions. Transmitting both positive and negative frequencies to the cells, creating a reaction within, be that opening and expanding to receive or to constrict and reduce the flow of nourishment.

Our heart centre is the balance and expression of our emotions, as we picture the heart; its functions are a balance of blood flowing in and out. It carries the blood, vital nutrients, oxygen and hormones to the body, and it receives and filters the blood to the lungs for oxygenation. It is the centre of giving and receiving.

Our heart receives these emotions to express and release, however, quite often through old beliefs and our environment, we withhold these emotions, we fear being open to a perceived vulnerability, the fear of rejection etc. You may have been brought up in an environment that people did not express their emotions freely, of love, joy, sadness, grief, becoming your patterns of being.

This suppression of emotions seen within our guardians is perceived as an absence in the eyes of a young child, even though the individuals would have been physically present, they were emotionally absent and detached, forging a disconnection a perceived belief of being unworthy of love and feeling rejected on certain levels.

This is especially true depending on our relationship to our Mother, within 3 weeks of the embryo forming, the heart beats giving life to these cells.

In the womb, our mother's blood comes into intimate contact with our blood through the placenta, carrying white and red cells, platelets and a complete impression of our genetic code, our DNA, providing us life and nourishment, as did her mother to her. The emotional state of our mother and her thoughts of her pregnancy, would have had strong imprinting into us growing within the womb through the connection of our blood.

Within our blood is our history, the old saying, "it's in their blood", through our blood we connect to our ancestors and their history, however, our blood is unique to us. We are a unique miracle in itself. Quite often blood issues are connected to family and ancestral issues as much as they are of individuality, where we may experience a loss of self or personal power.

When we block the flow of receiving and expression we restrict the cell walls of the capillaries, veins and arteries gradually forming physical restrictions, these tensions cause a reduction of flow. We build a barrier, a dam of emotions causing pressure, deprivation to other areas and stagnation.

Physically, we may see this as an imbalance of blood pressure affecting our circulation, hypertension, high cholesterol, heightened tension and pressure within oneself, most likely due to putting too much pressure on yourself, triggered as stress and anxiety.

Or in reverse, low blood pressure, the walls of the arteries, capillaries and veins are weakened, there is little of no energetic input, there is a withdrawal, a resistance to meet challenges, an inability to stand on your own without feeling weak or collapsing. Leading to ineptitude when confronting difficulties and taking responsibility of ones actions, easily feeling overwhelmed. This also correlates with our base chakra, on how supported and safe we feel, holding the strength and integrity within the body and musculoskeletal system.

In Tradition Chinese Medicine the heart meridian extends to the arms, knowing that the limbs are connected through the fascia and cells from the heart, this is seen in heart attacks, as weakness and pain is felt within the left arm.

Poor circulation seen ins Raynaud's disease, usually affects the extremities, the feet, hands, nose and ears, the parts that go out into the world first and farthest, the toes that point our direction of life, the fingers that reach out to touch and hold.

From my experience in clinics, I have seen patterns with those suffering from poor circulation, may also have lower back and sacral issues; menstrual pain and complications; a lack of libido; large intestine dysfunction. All lay within the sacral chakra, the well of emotions, as the element of water, which is the foundation of our blood, the fountain and sustaining source of life!

The physical restrictions in the sacral area impinge the blood flow through the abdominal aorta —common iliac and femoral arteries which supply the lower limbs and then back to the heart.

"I open my heart and arms to fully embrace the light of love to nourish my soul, my heart, my mind and my body"

Our arms are the extension of our heart, they are either open to receive and give love, think how we go to hug, we open our arms thus our hearts to receive the other persons embrace. To hold them tightly, our heart chakras connect to read and flow with one another's hearts and feelings through this open and expansive energy and frequency of love. Our heart and lungs take this hug enveloping and absorbing breath to receive this wonderful healing emotion, the sustenance of life.

Hugging those that we love and care for, it is an instinctive way of expressing and receiving love, to exchange the powerful emotion of love to one another with no requirements of words.

The unsaid words of; *"I Love you, I care for you, I am there for you, I support you"*. We open our hearts to each other, we breakdown walls; we hold a loving vulnerability yet so strong. In moments of life, all we need is a hug to help us feel better, lifted in spirits and feel supported in life.

Some hugs are just amazing, supportive and comforting, others are awkward and distant, more of a motion than an expression or feeling. Take a moment and visualise how you hug; do you hug people, are you a hugger, a Mr Tickle with those amazing enveloping arms, giving those you love a big squeeze, a bear hugger where people can nestle into your chest to feel safe and supported?

Do you lift people off the ground in your embrace, are you a hesitant hugger, or do you round the shoulders and back so the hearts do not completely connect, maybe a tentative pat-of-the-back to the other? Does hugging feel natural to you, or is it more of a social expectation that you feel you have to perform?

I am known to give a hug after my treatments, for me it's an exchange of kindness and care, a way of sending my clients out with a feeling of support and love.

I hug my children holding and breathing in their beauty, warmth and their smell, being in the moment of bliss holding these miracles I have been blessed with. I am always hugging people to say hi, it is my mission to hug a certain friend of mine, who, doesn't do hugs, probably most annoying but it makes her laugh! For me it is about opening the beauty of our hearts, our uniqueness that is a gift to the world.

Studies have shown how a 10-second hug helps the body fight infections, eases depression, and lessens tiredness. A 20-second hug reduces the harmful effects of stress, relieves blood pressure, and ensures a healthy heart, through release of oxytocin, a 60-second hug will boost not only oxytocin, yet also dopamine, your attachment and pleasure hormones.

I read once on social media (it has its benefits!), how hugging your children, rather than you pulling away after a few moments, just hold them until they decide to break free.

I did this and you will be amazed as to how long that cuddle can be! It actually feels like our hearts are recharging one another and regulating our nervous system. Often when my younger son would be *"acting out"*, I would say would you like a *Mummy Hug*, rather than responding to his mood, quite quickly he realised it was a hug that he needed to feel better – it has become a lighthearted thing now, no pun intended, however, it just shows how we can become deregulated and there are quick beautiful ways to get us back on track.

As pain follows the same neural pathways as loneliness, we can begin to understand how a hug can have so many healing benefits to our mind and body.

Open Our Hearts

Support your heart chakra by lovingly approving and accepting yourself, to know that we are never alone when we connect to our hearts, the universal frequency of love.

Open you heart to be your strength and to be your anchor in this world, to hold comfort and support, to feel safe and secure in this world.

To set yourself free from the fears and chains of rejection, to fully embrace and love yourself, your uniqueness, to know that you are a spectrum of light and love and to allow your light to shine brightly in this world, that has never needed it as much as it does now.

> "My Heart is my Anchor, my Love is my Strength"
> "I am loved"
> "I love myself unconditionally"
> "I forgive all and release myself from hurt and pain"
> "I welcome love with an open heart"
> "My heart is free from all the wounds of the past."
> "I forgive others, and I forgive myself."
> "I am open to love and receive more of it every day."
> "I naturally attract love everywhere I go."
> "I create supportive, loving relationships that are good for me."

I invite you to note any thoughts, understandings, aha moments.

_____
_____
_____
_____
_____
_____
_____
_____
_____
_____
_____
_____
_____
_____
_____
_____
_____
_____
_____
_____
_____
_____

21.

THROAT CHAKRA - VISHUDDHA "PURE"

Chakras of Communication
The upper three chakras are at the base of the throat, the centre of the forehead and above the crown of the head.
They are physically close to one another representing and regulating our communication with and our understanding with the world.
The Throat chakra is our means of expression of what we know and feel
The Brow/third eye chakra brings an awareness, insight and clarity of perception.
The Crown unites us individually and collectively to the world and universe.

Overview

The Throat Chakra – represents the element of space or ether, in Sanskrit the Akasha, the pure cosmic sound of creation, where all elements dissolve into their refined essence.

It carries the bija mantra Ham, which has a downward vibration from throat to heart, the clearing and opening of heart felt expression.

In the west it is represented by the colour of blue. Blue emits the energy of calmness, stability, and peace. It is the epitome of faith, truthfulness, reliability, support, confidence, and guidance. Our throat is about expression of truth and authenticity.

Our truth is a frequency, a tone and vibration that cuts through the white noise and felt to our core. When we hear someone speak their heart felt truth with passion and love, it resonates within, that forms a connection of integrity.

Cycle of Nature and development – the throat chakra expands from 7-12 years the pre-pubescent stage of life and expression, this is when we begin to find our voice and how to navigate the expression of our emotions.

If the foundations of the lower chakras have been nurtured, confidence is gained from a firm emotional base and through the throat, the individual feels safe in their voice and is able to express and give back to the family and community. This is often in plays and performances at school.

Physical Relationship – the fifth chakra, the throat, is located near the cervical vertebra and the base of the throat governing communication and creativity.

The cervical nerve plexus is located here, which consists of two groups, the muscular and sensory nerve branches, supplying the muscles of the neck, head and diaphragm.

Vital nerves served from the brain stem, for instance the Vagus nerve (CNX) which influences the larynx and tone of voice, and the pharyngeal nerve plexus, that regulates the mouth and throat are also found here.

The chakra includes the thyroid and parathyroid glands which control the body's metabolic rate and mineral levels. It relates to the absorption of key nutrients vital for our everyday lives and homeostasis, highlighting another boundary of discernment, to take what serves us and to release what doesn't, physically, emotionally and mentally.

Balance and optimum flow – following the foundation and development of the lower chakras of feeling safe and supported, self-love and self-acceptance, you are able to freely express oneself with your authentic truth with integrity and creativity.

Your emotions, feelings and understanding of oneself, others, and the environment and world in which you live in, are easily expressed with love and compassion with good intention for self and those around you.

Imbalance symptoms- If unbalanced, the throat chakra may physically represent in hypo or hyper active thyroid conditions; poor mineral absorption, fatigue, reduced bone density, which are similar to menopausal symptoms, throat goiters through lack of iodine absorption, hormone imbalance symptoms.

Emotionally, you may find it challenging to understand and express one's true emotions and feelings, often masking ourselves and pretending to be someone else that you perceive will be acceptable, often excessively shy and avoid speaking out for fear of rejection and the consequences.

Or if too open, individuals may talk too much, caught up in the gossip and drama, often complaining. Finding it hard to listen to others and to see deep within the narrative of what they are hearing. They may find it hard to connect to oneself blocking their creative side and expression of the soul.

Possible Symptoms-
- Hypo and hyperthyroidism
- Chronic Fatigue
- Regular sore throats/glandular fever
- Ears-nose-throat complications
- Headaches/Migraines
- Jaw tension – TMJ
- Head-neck and shoulder restrictions
- Snoring – also links to heart chakra
- Unable to express emotions nor understand your own emotions
- Find it hard to trust and make decisions, to discern what is the truth

"Words are Magic I speak them Magically"

The Vissuddha in Sanskrit means pure or purification, the Akashic pure cosmic sound that was the beginning of life. It is our energy centre that governs our ability to seek and speak our truth to ourselves and to express our emotional self to others. How we experience life has a strong correlation to the sound and frequency that we emit into the universe, what we say and what we do not. Our throat chakra allows us to access our deep internal truth, to experience a life filled with integrity and alignment to our joy, purpose and desires.

In nature the throat chakra would be the songs of the birds, the calling of the owls, the buzzing of the insects, the howls of the wolves and the roaring of the lions. Each are an expression of connection, of love and support, of warning and safety.

Think of the cry of help from a tiny cub for its mother, the cry of an infant help and nurturing in return is received; the calling rituals of animals, birds and insects for a mate; the classic image of a man serenading to a woman, this vulnerable expression of love for another for one to receive in return.

Our bodies are dense forms of energy, and as energy attracts energy, the frequency of our thoughts and words that we express are what we receive.

"I freely speak with love, self-acceptance, honesty and integrity"

Our voice is established when we are born, the instinctive cry for breath opening up the throat, thorax and lungs. The instinctive cry and noises of an infant is about communicating their needs essential for survival and connection, part of the challenge as a parent is to understand.

The high pitched shrill of anxiety when they are scared that makes your heart jump and pull towards them, to give a loving touch, cradled in love to know they are safe. The grumpy hunger cry preceding the burst of noises, that becomes more frequent if ignored, to provide the nourishment of food, satisfaction and a loving connection often with the mother through the nurture of the breast; the painful cry of wind and the happy giggles and snuffles when they look for interaction and connection.

Although our throat chakra initially develops during the ages of 7 years to 12 years, the pre-pubescent years in terms of language and self-expression, our basic understanding of cause and effect are learnt throughout our early years from day one.

As a baby, if we had all our nurturing and survival needs taken care of efficiently by our guardians, we would have learnt that our voice is a powerful tool. The first words normally around 11-13 months, the baby sees and establishes this connection further, hopefully rewarded with positive reinforcement of attention and smiles of encouragement.

Building and transitioning into the toddler years, the tantrums often stemmed from lack of being able to communicate what they like, and also not getting what they want, depending on the supportiveness of the boundaries that have been established, the cheeky smiles that wins over the hearts to get that treat or extra playtime.

Following into the early school years, interacting with their peers and how communication and understanding of one's place and others in this environment, creating their own boundaries of acceptable behaviour of what they will and will not tolerate.

We can therefore see how our early years affect how we express ourselves, be they of support, nurturing emotionally, receiving love and acceptance in abundance. Creating an open and balanced throat chakra, or one more of suppression, should one's voice of cries were not heard as a baby.

If one wasn't nurtured, comforted, nourished and loved, the foundations of the fundamental elements of the first four chakras are more fragile. To feel safe and supported and the belonging of the base chakra; our emotional needs, joy and sweetness of the sacral chakra; the fire, warmth and nourishment of our bellies of self-acceptance of the solar plexus and the unconditional embrace and balance of love within the heart chakra.

> *"All my relationships in my life are a reflection of love, respect, acceptance, honesty and kindness"*

A lack of nurture and positive reinforcement, may create patterns and beliefs that one's voice is of no use, that no one listens anyway. To feel one is not worthy of love and acceptance, nor supported and safe, which may later be compounded by an overpowering and controlling parent and/or authoritative figures; only allowing their viewpoint to be heard, believed and followed, Such as the old belief system that states *"children are to be seen and not heard"*; which may create a pattern and belief later in the individual's life and adulthood, that to be heard is to be of a voice with an overpowering force, highly opinionated and not necessarily open to other angles of thought.

Likewise yet more subtly, children are like sponges, constantly reading and absorbing the environment around them, be that of thought and behavioural patterns and beliefs, the spoken and the unspoken words and the energetic frequencies of their guardians. A parent may hold little self-love and acceptance, constantly criticising how they look, never being happy with oneself, seeking approval and reassurance from others.

However, as a parent they try to teach their child self-love by saying how lovely they look. What the child hears and absorbs are the patterns of self-criticism, a belief that your worth is based upon your looks, they mirror the inward rejection of self, the self-sabotage.

Another example of learning through "osmosis", would be the dynamic of the parents' close relationships, which may be imbalanced, one parent's voice is not heard, or they do not stand up for themselves, seeking "peace" to avoid disharmony or worse violence. The parent sacrifices their peace to keep the peace, a people pleasing pattern.

Again, the parent may try to teach the child otherwise, yet the words they speak or do not to themselves and others, are the patterns and beliefs that the child inherits deep within their psyche. Such as, it is ok to not take responsibility for your anger and emotions; it is other's roles to absorb, to keep the peace, to be a martyr-victim, fuelling abusive relationships to continue in generations to come.

The liver is the sponge to such toxic environments; a child will believe the environment has something to do with them. They absorb the anger; they become more alert and triggered by loud noises and voices, subconsciously reading the environment to know if they are safe; what we would term Empathic.

This is something I acknowledge within myself, however, now that I am more conscious of, I actually see this empathy and being able to read and absorb others emotions as a gift in my ability as a healer.

The key is discernment, what is mine and what is theirs, rather than taking on as my own – I can read the emotional state and alchemise. However, this has taking my lifetime to become conscious and understand this – regular self-care and connection to self is fundamental to cleanse and clear, and recognise my emotional state. Boundaries and Discernment – the fundamental principles of health and wellbeing

Bringing us full circle to about understanding the frequency that we emit through the words we speak to ourselves and to the external world, being the light we wish to see in this world, to be the light for others to look towards.

"I am a beacon of love and creativity"
"I lovingly approve and accept my true self"

Our truth is an orchestra of senses that resonates within- The throat chakra is our teacher, the conductor of the orchestra that allows us to bring depth to our experiences and life's journey. If we only heard one voice, one opinion, one tone, the sound of life would be limited and restricted. Yet, when we listen to various voices and all of the beautiful frequencies that emanate from the orchestra as a whole, we create a beautiful symphony of depth, diversity and expansive energy, working through our entire being.

Our frequency of truth is a creation from all of our senses, the chakras integrate to hold the notes of our senses, the smells, tastes, sight, hearing and touch recorded within the limbic system our mind and brow chakra; the crown our connection to the universe; our heart and gut intuition to process all these senses; feeling and emotions of the sacral, without such, our truth and throat chakra has nothing tangible to hold onto.

As we develop through the initial stages of the throat chakra around the pre-pubescent years of 7-12, we are generally exposed to opinions, beliefs and patterns. Quite often teaching is about repetition, the constant beat of the drum, until whatever we are being taught finally registers "sinks in". How often do we hear a child asking why? With the common response of "it just is!".

A child of these years may come to accept and believe all information and beliefs passed down by generations. Even though they may sense conflict within, they are unable to express effectively, if the environment doesn't allow to be explored, becoming their truth and beliefs.

These accepted yet not resonated truths, causes uncertainty of self and more complex inner beliefs later in ones' journey, a tangle of uncertainty and lack of trust of oneself and emotions. These deep intuitive feelings of our heart centre and solar plexus are often overridden by the head, manifesting physically as restriction and inflammation within the heart and gut, we begin to see the trail and layers that are to be unpeeled, for us to get to the root of our individual healing journeys.

However, when we are in a supportive and nourishing environment, of open debate and free speech, we explore these various beliefs, not fearing reactions and ridicule in expressing a new way of thinking. Not to be seen as controversial, simply explorative and to experience through all our senses through play.

Debate is fundamental and required to develop attitudes of flexibility and tolerance within our society. The growth of us as an individual and the collective society and civilisation, are based upon being able to hear and process the thoughts of those around; to hold respect and acceptance of self and each other, sharing a uniting of dreams and desires that serve all to the highest good.

Think of science and how this has evolved into what we feel are our truths now, yet many forward thinking scientists in their lifetime were ridiculed for their findings at the time. However, several years, decades' evens centuries later, it gradually becomes accepted as the new truth and belief.

An example would be Charles Darwin, his Theory of Natural Selection flew in the face and the beliefs of God and was rejected. Today, we still have this lack of acceptance of other viewpoints, hypothesis, and revolutionary findings when it brings uncertainty and change to the current known "control" of present beliefs in many aspects of our society, especially in the Health and Medicine Industry.

Hippocrates had the holistic approach to health, understanding the causes and the person not the symptoms. It is only becoming more recognised and accepted that our health depends on the health of our gut, Hippocrates lived in 460BCE- and we think of ourselves as advanced!

> "All disease begins in the gut."
> "It is far more important to know what person the disease has than what disease the person has."
> "Before you heal someone, ask him if he's willing to give up the things that make him sick."
> "Natural forces within us are the true healers of disease."
> — Hippocrates

We may find ourselves going full circle and understand it is our choices, environment and emotions that affects our health, all of which we can become aware of and make the changes should we wish to. To recognise that our health is actually in our hands and to be empowered with such, when we seek the holistic approach, the cause not the symptom, we have the opportunity to heal.

Therefore, being open to listen and to receive other angles of thought is paramount to our evolution, both individually and collectively, in our society and globally.

Language is our evolutionary leap that has developed in a way that we are able to communicate beyond our instinctive and primal ways to share knowledge, concepts and experiences. It has given us the ability to understand what is happening to others that are around us and in the world. It also brings us more into our minds, of the past and the future and less frequently in the present moment.

Therefore, it is imperative for our health to create space for our thoughts and experiences. To allow the mind to quieten, to process our emotions and reactions, to seek what does not serve us joy, to seek our inner truth and authentic self and light.

Holding objectivity and being the observer of self, enables us to let go of these old ways and emotions that have weighed us down. We become lighter, more joyful, sharing ones' light and authentic self and in the flow of life, the beautiful gift of wisdom when we allow our unique light to shine.

Our reflection of life is our perception

The environment, in which the child grows up in, becomes the foundation and structure of the throat chakra and one's own belief systems. Influencing how and what we hear, creating perceptions of experiences throughout life.

These often play out as triggers, as an adult we may react to current situations yet hearing and seeing it from an old wound as a 5 year old. Being told they were not good enough and constantly told off or punished; now suddenly, they are overwhelmed by a situation at work, where the boss is highlighting areas of concern or required improvement.

This challenge and situation could easily be perceived differently. If the child had been positively encouraged whilst growing up, the adult may see this interaction with the boss, not as a reflection of their capability, yet see it as a situation to grow.

Likewise, traumas and emotionally challenging situations experienced as an adult, can also be triggers later in life. However, these may be more conscious patterns to the individual than the earlier foundation experiences. Self-reflection may highlight similar repeating patterns.

Understanding why we perceive situations and act in certain ways, through indirect or direct experiences, is a matter of gentle unpeeling of the emotional and physical layers. Once we hold awareness of these old serving patterns, beliefs and fears, we then can start the healing process of unraveling in a kind, compassionate space.

"I speak from my heart filled with love and compassion to the highest good for all"

Creating flow, balance and homeostasis

"Through self-love and acceptance, I speak peacefully and in flow with my emotions and feelings"

The chakra is represented by the colour and hues of blue, which our minds and body are neurologically hardwired to promoting calm and peace. If you picture the sun setting during the twilight hours you have pale blues, purples and violets, (all the colours of the chakras of communication). Preparing us to unwind, to slow down, to come into a restful state, ready for sleep.

As the light reduces, objects become less visible; our mental activity is reduced, creating an objective detachment to enable us to contemplate the day and how we would wish the following day to be, gradually descending into a more imaginative, vague, peaceful and dreamlike state.

A true sense of peace arises, when there is equilibrium and flow within the whole chakra system. The throat is vital for this balance supporting each of the other chakras to open and release.

The throat chakra is represented by the element of space, the etheric template body upon which contains and incorporates all of the elements, earth, water, fire and air, the lower four chakras.

The throat is the control centre, similar to a release valve, allowing the outward flow and release of energy, through communication and expression. A buildup of energy from the other chakras and areas of our bodies creates pressure; the areas of high pressure come to the surface, releasing to allow balance to occur.

When this release process is restricted, the pressure is exerted into other areas of the body and major energy centres. Going up to the brow/third eye chakra where one tends to live in one's world of fantasy, and possibly trying to ignore and exclude from reality. Especially if the environment was toxic when growing up, an old coping survival mechanism. The example of the above, would possibly be when the child feels their voice is hopeless or unheard, to go within oneself, closing the throat and one's expression

Equally, it may also do the opposite, pushing downwards to the survival base and emotional sacral chakra, and the boundaries of the solar plexus, our centre of processing. This may be seen as excessive manipulation of others in covert or overt aggression, without one's own awareness of such behavioural patterns.

When we are in the presence of fear, we never fully speak our truth. Due to our experiences we may even be so disconnected from our heavy emotions of grief, guilt and shame, that we close down,

Subconsciously fearful of what may be released, and the potential of reliving the event and trauma, weighs heavy and constricts to a cellular level.

We may fear rejection of the perceived consequences of speaking out, speaking one's mind if different to others. This may have evolved from one's life experiences, and/ or the invisible parameters of social conditioning, supported by the media and social platforms.

Shame certainly blocks us from speaking our truth, victims of abuse, take on what I see as the shame of the perpetrator as their own. It is this shame that closes one down, unable to express our truth, for the fear of rejection! From my experience, truth can feel like a chaotic, healing, fusion bomb!

A times, I have had the quiet whispers saying to me "your truth will set you free" – my response to that was, great thanks a lot, as I could feel the dread within me! However, I have lived this now for several years much more consciously, and as much as it scares the *shit* out of you at times, it really does set you free – even amongst the tornado of chaos!

At times I felt, I was the eye of the storm, rooted to the trust in my truth, there was actually a sense of calm and peace within this storm of transformation! Highlighting how imperative it is to have regular grounding practice, so you stay on your axis, and regulate your nervous system.

"I am safe in the power of my love and acceptance of self to speak my truths"

In the words of Brené Brown, *"Shame is Universal, we all have it!"* It can range from abuse, our sexuality, sex itself, self-pleasure, our desires, money, being made redundant, infertility, our mental health and our family.

What makes shame grow is judgement of self, the fear of judgement from others, secrecy and silence. Brené states that communication and *"Empathy is the Antidote",* self-compassion being part of that. To be objective, and to step out of the downward spiral of shame, to observe more consciously, out of our primal survival behaviours. Self-love and acceptance is the space that enables this higher perspective and to be able to process and heal.

> *The wonderful thing about Lotus*
> *Is that it is impervious to the swamp*
> *Even after growing in murky waters*
> *It remains clean and has a neoteric stamp.*
>
> Lotus by Chandra Thiagarajan

When we are in the pure energy of trust, love and acceptance we begin to unfold like a lotus flower sharing our beauty, truth and vulnerability. We do this as we heal through our chakras, a healthy base chakra and foundation to truly feel that one belongs in this world, to feel safe and supported in ourselves; deepening a level of trust of our innate wisdom, the solar and heart; our visceral reactions become indicators as to whether we are in alignment to our joy, sacral, and our truth, our heart and throat.

From this space of connection and awareness to self and our body, we are able to step up in our truth, authenticity and joy.

> *"All is well; everything is working out for my highest good"*
> Louise Hay

In or out?

Physically the throat and pharynx control the in and out breath and what we consume. The pharynx, is a passageway that extends from the base of the skull, to the level of the sixth cervical vertebrae, serving both the respiratory and digestive systems, by receiving air from the nasal cavity and air, food, and water from the oral cavity.

As we know, we are unable to breathe in and swallow at the same time, otherwise we would choke. Nor are we able to speak properly on the in breath. We speak as the air from our lungs pass through the larynx and throat, creating the tone and frequency of our voice. It is through intricate and precise co-ordination of nerves and muscles, which enables us to perform such delicate functions, with minimal conscious thought.

It is the cranial Vagus nerve that regulates the tone of our voices, which is unique to each of us, just like our thumbprints. Those that have a monotone voice may well have poor vagal nerve functionality. Practicing toning, mantra meditations including the mantra OM are very effective in improving your vagal tone.

The Vagus nerve is accessible around the throat and neck as it travels from the brain, to the jugular foramen behind the ears, running parallel to the common carotid artery and the sternocleidomastoid (SCM) neck muscle, to the sternoclavicular joint, where our throat meets our sternum/ breastbone.

One way to release tensions of the vagus nerve is by stretching your ear lobes and opening your jaw, you'll be amazed by how much tension is held here!

The throat chakra encompasses the ears and, the sphenoid bone, a cranial bone deep within the skull, often called the Angel Bone. It is what gives the structure of the upper palate of our mouths, supports the brain and creates the lower part of the ear canal. Restrictions from birth and or head traumas, including whiplash, will present tensions here.

The auricular communication branch of the vagus nerve, connects to the Glossopharyngeal nerve IX, extending to the pharyngeal plexus. Collectively, they regulate and control all aspects of our throat, mouth, ears and nose.

For instance, the stylopharyngeal muscle is responsible for elevating the larynx and pharynx, especially during speaking and swallowing; sensory innervation to the tongue, affecting our taste and palate. The carotid sinus and body regulates the blood pressure and chemoreceptors; the two small tubes (Eustachian tubes) which connect the middle ears to the pharynx, and allow air pressure on the eardrum to be equalized. Any inflammation would cause earaches and hearing difficulties.

There are many nerves that branch and connect with the vagus nerve extending to our whole visceral system. Any restrictions in the neck, throat and occipital area through trauma and injury, such as whiplash, falls, poor posture, the classic posture we see now with high usage of phones, from bacterial and viral infections; stress and tension can reduce the optimum function of the Vagus nerve, and will affect the whole of our bodies regulation and healing.

Due to its intricate pathways through the neck, it supports the idea that the throat chakra is the control valve and regulating centre of the lower chakras.

Within the neck and throat area, the phrenic nerve. whose most important role is serving the diaphragm, the prime muscle for respiration, receives innervation from the cervical and brachial plexus.

The cervical plexus innervates the muscles of the neck, and the brachial plexus extending to the shoulder and arms. The phrenic nerve journey innervates the mediastinal pleura, a thin membrane between the chest cavity and the area between the lung and the pericardium - a fibrous sac that encloses the heart and great vessels. It keeps the heart in a stable location in the mediastinum, facilitates its movements, and separates it from the lungs and other mediastinal structures.

Damage and/or restrictions of the phrenic nerve can be from posture, upper chest breathing overusing the accessory respiratory muscles which are mostly in the neck, mainly the scalenes as the nerve runs alongside the anterior scalene; injury, Lyme's Disease, neurological diseases such as cervical spondylosis and multiple sclerosis. The symptoms range from minor hiccups to diaphragmatic dysfunction.

"Every day I am in the flow and balance of receiving of what I need and letting go of all that I do not"

The Thyroid

The most notable organs of the throat are the thyroid and parathyroid. They are endocrine glands, which govern metabolism of the muscles, heart and digestive system, growth and development of the brain and body.

It is innervated by the Vagus nerve, with connection to the voice box/larynx, the recurrent laryngeal nerve. The thyroid and parathyroid glands produce three hormones that regulate these functions, by releasing these hormones within the blood system, namely, triiodothyronine, also known as T3, tetraiodothyronine, also called thyroxine or T4, and calcitonin.

Depending on our activity and stress, our bodies need more thyroid hormones, and sometimes they need less. To regulate the correct level of hormones, the thyroid gland is controlled by the pituitary gland, which in turn is regulated by the hypothalamus that forms part of our limbic system, highlighting the intrinsic relationship of our emotions and hormones.

Iodine is one of the main building blocks of both T3 and T4 hormones. Our bodies cannot produce this trace element, so we need to get enough of it in our diet. Iodine is absorbed into our bloodstream from food in our large intestine; it is then carried to the thyroid gland, where it is eventually used to make thyroid hormones.

The absence of which results in goiters/nodules and hypothyroidism. This highlights the importance of our gut health to support its many functions of absorption of key minerals and vitamins for our health. The only other organ that comes close to the thyroid's use of iodine is the prostate.

Many symptoms of an underactive thyroid (hypothyroidism), are the same as those of other conditions, so it can easily be confused for something else. Symptoms usually develop slowly, often not recognising that there is an imbalance.

Symptoms of hypothyroidism may include:
Tiredness - Being sensitive to cold - Weight gain – Constipation – Depression - Slow movements and thoughts - Muscle aches and weakness - Muscle cramps - Dry and scaly skin - Brittle hair and nails

- Loss of libido (sex drive) – Pain – Numbness, and a tingling sensation in the hand and fingers (carpal tunnel syndrome) - Irregular periods or heavy periods.

Women are ten times likely to suffer from hypothyroidism than men and may exacerbate menopausal symptoms. Elderly people with an underactive thyroid may develop memory problems and depression. Children may experience slower growth and development. Teenagers may start puberty earlier than normal.

The opposite is a hyperthyroidism, where there are too many thyroid hormones being produced, over stimulating the cells and the metabolism. It can be trigger by Graves disease, an autoimmune disorder and inflammation, all of which link back to the health of the gut and the vagus nerve.

Symptoms of hyperthyroidism may include:

Nervousness, anxiety and irritability; Mood swings; Difficulty sleeping; Persistent tiredness and weakness; Sensitivity to heat; Swelling in your neck from an enlarged thyroid gland (goitre); An irregular and/or unusually fast heart rate (palpitations); Twitching or trembling; Insomnia; Weight loss; Frequent bowel movement/diarrhea; Changes in menstrual cycle (usually shorter cycle, lighter periods)

Things to consider to improve one's thyroid function and health, is your fluoride intake and exposure. Fluoride is found in water, levels dependent upon the area and Water Company, and mouth hygiene products such as toothpaste.

It is known that fluoride is more electronegative than iodine, which easily displaces iodine within the body, thereby affecting the absorption and functioning of the thyroid gland. In other words, fluoride blocks our fundamental absorption of iodine, and thus affects our thyroid and prostrate health. Later I also highlight how this effects the health of the pineal gland.

Akasha

The pure cosmic sound of creation, where all elements dissolve into their refined essence.

The throat chakra encompasses all elements and the whole of the body, regulating and controlling the main functions of our health, balance and flow of the elemental chakras. To receive the nourishment that it needs to sustain life and the release of what no longer serves purpose or joy.

For a healthy balanced throat chakra, we need to hold space and awareness, to gain the understanding of our emotional layers, of the silent words and the internal narrative we speak to ourselves.

The connection to our emotional centres, the sacral and heart chakra are balanced through the attention to our spoken and unspoken words to our external world. Seeking our deep internal truths, our gut instinctive and heart felt wisdom, unpeeling the old behavioural patterns and thought processes that trigger our perceptions and actions.

A scientist called Dr Masaru Emoto found, that when certain words with emotions and feelings were spoken to water, through photographing the crystallisation of the various water experiments. The results were a variety of crystals, ranging from the most beautiful symmetrical patterns, to erratic dysfunctional shapes. The water that was immersed with love and gratitude was the most spectacular crystal, the one of hate had no pattern or crystal and was chaotic.

As our bodies are 70% water, our health is subject to the internal narrative we speak to ourselves and the words we allow to penetrate our boundaries. To transition towards a higher resonance and frequency of love, joy and gratitude is healing in itself.

Visualise the old expressions and sayings which highlight this functionality creating a picture as to how it may affect our body.

"A bitter pill to swallow" the suppressed and unexpressed anger and bitterness of how one was treated relates to the organ of the liver, and overflows to the gallbladder as storage. One of the liver's many

functions, are to create the bitter digestive enzyme bile, which is fundamental for our absorption of the nutrients we consume.

Liver dysfunction can be a result of a restricted throat chakra, an overflow of unexpressed anger, resentment, frustration, rage, which often refers to a tight jaw and teeth, as the jaw is clamped closed. The fear of expression, the belief that our words and feelings are not being heard or valued, stemming from childhood and/or other experiences later in life.

"To jump down ones throat", creates an image of closing that persons throat and becoming overpowered swallowing the others overt emotions and beliefs. Breaking through and invading the individual's personal energetic and emotional boundaries. Our physical boundaries are initially our skin, the first form of defense- our energetic boundary is the crown, our intentions.

The throat chakra is what we choose to swallow, literally and figuratively, which then leads into the gut-brain barrier. Fed from the throat, to the oesophagus and then into the stomach and digestive tract, which is the internal boundary, the last checking system before the blood-brain barrier.

"Too much to stomach" this is when we have become too open and consuming to outside influences, people's opinions, the news, an overload of work, *"bitten off more you can chew"* –not saying NO .

The throat chakra is fundamental to this – to express our boundaries and what serves us, to be able to discern what we listen and expose ourselves to.

For the stomach is our relationship with our social world – if our throat is weak and closed, we absorb and do not release, which most likely are not even ours to take on in the first place! This increases the levels of toxicity in the mind and body, emotionally and physically.

This is what I felt resonated to me through my early experiences of bulimia, the act of making myself sick, was a subconscious way of releasing something from within me, on a deep emotional and mental level.

The gut-brain barrier is what stands between any toxins we consume, to the blood and our central nervous system. It is also fundamental to our absorption of the key minerals and vitamins to maintain our health and wellbeing. We can then see how these defense boundary systems can become weakened, if constantly exposed to toxicity on all energetic levels.

Symptoms of skin disorders, poor mineral absorption and deficiency, fatigue and tiredness, auto immune and inflammatory diseases, can relate to the imbalance of the throat chakra and its relationship with the solar plexus

"Going for the jugular" – as detailed earlier, the jugular foramen is where the vital Vagus and glossopharyngeal nerve exit from the brain in to the neck, which are vital to all our senses and can actually cause unconsciousness from a specific blow to this area.

To "have a *"lump in the throat"* is the build-up of emotion from one's sacral and heart energy centre causing a restricted expression of crying.

"Singing ones praises" – this conjures an image of high vibrational powerful and positive energy, to sing, the throat, heart and lungs are open, releasing the frequencies of love and joy.

To be *"held by ones throat"* means unable to move or express one's thoughts, the startled state of fear closing the larynx.

In summary, as part of our healing journey, balancing the throat chakra is equally important as the other elemental chakras. However, to heal and balance the other chakras, the intrinsic relationship with the throat of listening, receiving and expressing, the act of release and finding one's truths, are imperative to the homeostasis of our mind and body.

Every day, science is showing how we are energetic beings, and energy moves in frequency, of light and sound. Our emotions are the energy-in-motion, each with a frequency of their own.

Even the key atoms that create us, such as hydrogen, which comprises 75% of the known mass of the universe, has its own frequency of 440hz, A above middle C.

How different music resonates with us, is this down to our own frequency which aligns to our natural flow, coherence and oscillation? A particular style or song, just moves you, you have to get up and dance, feel the beat and smile. Or a tune that moves you to tears!

I believe, that we can heal our mind and bodies through finding our truth, our pure frequency and vibration that is unique to us. To be that truth, integrity and resonance – for when we do, all of our energetic bodies align, flow and communicate in a coherence, where everything is expanding and contracting as one, the most beautiful symphony!

Just like the tone of our voice and thumbprint that is unique to us, so is our purpose, our joy, our gifts, a blueprint that holds all that we are and our pure potential.

Opening and balancing our throat chakra, enables us to connect to all that we are. Through toning, stimulating and balancing our vagus nerve, practicing OM mantra and sacred chants, and living to our aligned desires and conscious choices, we draw upon this universal blueprint.

We call it to ourselves, to experience, feel and be, to resonate within the field that we choose-.

That my dear Soul, is empowerment, it is freedom, it breaks us free from all of the invisible ceilings placed upon us, we open into the field of pure unconscious potential, which is beyond our minds conceivability!

"A seed may lay within the Earth for eons, until the right moment environment presents itself
An environment that embodies the nourishment of trust and growth!"

Affirmations:
"I speak with love and integrity"
"I speak with love and truth"
"I freely speak with authenticity and creativity"
"I express my pure inner truth with love and self-acceptance"
"I speak within the frequency of humility"
"I communicate confidently and with ease."

"I am safe to speak from my heart."
"I am balanced in speaking and listening."
"I am safe to express my desires."
"I speak my true thoughts with ease."
"I have healthy boundaries"
"I am SAFE to feel and speak my truth"
"My feelings and voice are worthy to be heard"

I invite you to journal your thoughts...

22.

PRELUDE TO THE BROW AND CROWN CHAKRAS
A Personal Message

Before you read on into the brow and crown chakra chapters, I wish to share my journey of writing them and the in-between.

Each aspect of this content throughout the chakras which I started in early 2020 (the first lockdown) are my own healing. Every part was for me to comprehend and reflect inwards, to put the ground work in, I had to live and breathe my words first, to walk the talk as it were!

Interestingly, my ego decided then, that I would have all my writing completed by the early summer, and a course ready to launch, giving myself only a few months! I am now having a little chuckle to myself as I write this prelude two years later, now fully aware of this pattern of mine.

How I choose to create a constant drive and place huge pressure on myself to achieve, setting unrealistic goals, whether consciously or not, forms part of my un-serving patterns of self-sabotage. I somehow manage to take something of potential beauty and a gift for myself, into a negative overwhelm and dread, that completely blocks the joy from this opportunity of experiences!

I have grown to be aware of this pattern within my spiritual journey and self-exploration, I recognise this as a pathway of self-worth and inner trust, of self and the universe. Which we are all a part of, and is a part of us, a universal field of magick, mystery and wonder, to be explored with curiosity and courage.

Learning experiences are all stepping stones towards beholding our inner power. I am learning (as we never stop) the art of surrender, to trust in self and the universe of potentiality, knowing that I am enough when I lean in deep, to show up in this world, fully as myself, with love and acceptance. Aware of my fears and shadows, acknowledging that they are a part of me, yet choosing them not to define me, nor allow to cover my light, the essence of who I am and what I have, to share in this world.

The greater the inner depth of shadow work, enables the space for our light to shine even brighter to experience a fuller life of joy, love, inner peace and contentment in abundance. To inspire others to do the same, to finally realise our fears are an illusion, and are NOT worth what we are missing out of!

Navigating the paradox of courage and vulnerability through the conscious power of our hearts, held within self-love and acceptance, in a place of observation and awareness, we fully empower and open our life to abundance.

Life is about choices, when we make them consciously, with the curiosity to expand, and the courage to be vulnerable, we step up and into our power, and become our most strongest!

When I experienced my various perceived "delays" in my writing, it was always an opportunity to dive deeper into self and heal. There was a significant gap in writing the last two chapters, the brow and the crown chakras. I recognise this was another layer of fear, the fear of getting it right, of it being enough and how it would be perceived and received by others.

I started writing the brow and came to an abrupt stop, every time I tried, I blocked, to the point it became a chore not a joy, I was trying too hard, I had my creativity and intuition in a stranglehold!

I was trying to include far too much science, as science is deemed as acceptable and perceived as our truth. Yet science evolves! If we relied purely on science to tell us what our truth is, we would not know much, until "someone" else told us something new.

When we look at science this way, we can see how we become too heavily reliant upon it, and feel it is only our truth. We are disconnecting from our own internal wisdom, becoming fragmented, unbalanced, misaligned and disempowering ourselves, as we rely on others to tell us what our truth is.

Now I am most grateful for this delay, as the content would not have been the true healing energy to share with you, the old pattern of extreme push and drive against ones truth!

With this awareness, I then had a very powerful message and

instruction to write this preface for the last two chakras, to lay bare my fears of not being and doing enough, my vulnerabilities, the then lack of trust in self and the universe. The message was –

"The content needs to be what is not already out there, it needs to be different, it needs to challenge you and others in yours and their beliefs and patterns, to give our magick back, and how to empower people with their own inner power. How to reclaim back our own power and that is through our intuition, we can sit all day long in our logical brain, however, that blocks us, and we can sit heavily in our emotional reactive brain, and that blocks us too!."

This is about curiosity and courage to be vulnerable, to dance that paradox is when we grow. When we gift ourselves the choice of curiosity and courage to be vulnerable, breaking free from the need of acceptance, the need for perfection, giving us that moment that may feel contracted and fearful, actually gives us that huge expansion as a person and as a Soul.

Hence the writing from this point forward will be the dance of the "known", the "un-known" and the mystical, to challenge our perceptions, our perceived truths, to connect to all of our senses, to find our natural state of balance and wholeness, of inner peace, love and joy.

The brow and crown are intrinsic to one another in how our systems function from our perception, which is fed through our beliefs, patterns and emotions, consciously and subconsciously. The next two chapters will flow and intertwine, to understand how we are interacting with our internal thoughts and how that makes us act in our lives. How we are interacting with this energy field and universal matrix, the expansive energy field of potential, that we can navigate through when in a higher vibration of inner trust, love and acceptance.

Enjoy reading and I sincerely hope you are rekindled with your inner magick, your beautiful and miraculous spirit and soul.

"Everything I Need is Already Within Me"

23.

BROW CHAKRA – AJNA
"To Command"

"Today and every day, I am the best person I can be, living and creating my true potential"

Overview

The Brow Chakra – symbolises the unified consciousness of the combined male and female deity – unconditional truth – both the Ida and Pingala (Nadis) – becoming one and connecting to the Sushmana, the life force and connection to Source. It signifies the end of duality and unity as one.

The sound to activate the third eye in mantra is Aum mantra (pronounced ah-uu-mm). It is a sacred sound considered by many ancient philosophical texts, the sound of the universe, encompassing all other sounds within it.

The colours represented by the brow chakra are indigo and purple. Theses are colours and light of clarity, similar to the throat chakra of blue, indigo and purple calm the mind, softening the eyes and our external vision. To come within ourselves with conscious awareness of self, seeking a higher perspective, vision and truth, held in our meta-consciousness, a state of objectivity to review, reflect, revaluate and release.

The Cycle of Nature and development – The brow chakra begins to open and expand in our adolescence, as a young person, we are encouraged to reflect on patterns in our lives and others, seeking our truth and values.

This is the first of the several key stages when it is possible to reinvent and readjust our role, as an individual in the collective of the world.

In the lower chakras, psychic messages tend to be more visceral feelings and knowing, our gut instincts and senses, whereas, the third eye is received more as an insight.

Physical Relationship– The brow chakra is located at the centre of the forehead and is linked to the neuroendocrine pineal gland. The gland is fundamental for the regulation of our circadian rhythm, the cycles of rest and repair, and our daily activity and growth. It is the top of the chain of the whole endocrine system.

The related organs are the eyes, and both hemispheres of the brain and the sinuses.

The key nerves are the external carotid plexus, which is a combination of postganglionic (running from) sympathetic fibres, derived from the Superior Cervical Ganglion (SCG) plexus. The external carotid plexus plays an important role in innervating the mid and lower face.

The Basal Ganglia, our subconscious, the basement of our brain, refers to a group of subcortical nuclei, responsible primarily for motor control, as well as other roles such as motor learning, executive functions and behaviours, and emotions.

The Suprachiasmatic Nucleus (SCN), is a bilateral structure located in the anterior part of the hypothalamus. It is the central pacemaker of the circadian timing system, and regulates most circadian rhythms in the body alongside the pineal gland

Optic Nerve CNII, the nerve that carries messages from the retina to the brain.

Balance and optimum flow – the chakra relates to our intuition, wisdom and spiritual awareness, the seeing clearly with perspective and equilibrium, a reality in balance of the logical and the intuitive. To be able to have an intuition and insight of situations from a higher perspective, forming an inner truth, derived from the collective of our senses.

To bridge our sixth sense with an understanding in coherence with our heart, to focus our energy and intentions to what we wish to feel and be. Harnessing the ability to visualise these heart felt desires from within, into the outer world, the inner magick and power of manifestation.

To be able to view the physical outer world clearly, yet also living within trust of one's inner wisdom, and knowing one's direction and soul purpose in life, holding a strong moral compass.

Imbalance –May find it difficult to see the bigger picture of one's life, struggling to re-evaluate and see new ways of thought processes. Feel unable to break un-serving patterns in one's life, a sense of not being able to find a way out, a sense of hopelessness.

If weak/closed/damaged –Tends to be an overly practical brain, creativity doesn't come easily. Holds more restrictive thought patterns and won't be swayed, unable to see the bigger picture and quite often narrow minded and dismissive of other's opinions. Most likely detached from spirituality and find it difficult to visualise.

Maybe successful with external and material wealth, however, may feel an inner lacking or purpose, an emptiness that you are unable to figure out why.

Too open/ over developed - Often feel overwhelmed or confused and struggle to concentrate or plan ahead, can be out of touch with reality, superstitious, suffering with feelings of delusion and paranoia.

Often lives in a fantasy world and unable to bring visions into reality. This may also be due to imbalance in other chakras such as the solar plexus, of scattered thoughts and the base chakra of being grounded, especially if experienced trauma in life, as a coping mechanism of separation to self. –

Often lose touch with reality and has obsessive hallucinations.

Physical Imbalance – When experiencing endocrine, hormone health issues, the third eye is fundamental as it is the command centre of the neuroendocrine system. The pineal gland regulates the pituitary gland that links to the Crown chakra.

The pituitary gland is the messenger and transmitter to the whole of the body, following the choice and perception from the pineal gland. The pattern breaker is whether it has come from conscious thoughts held from multiple senses, or from the subconscious mind, the basal ganglion, and the unconscious body, beholding our deep belief systems.

Our health relies upon the nervous and endocrine system; they are the regulators of rest and restore, our energy levels and the ability to function. Therefore, all health issues will come back to the brow and crown chakras, however, key symptoms that mostly relate to the brow are;

- Brain fog, find it hard to concentrate, indecision and memory recall if too open
- Tiredness and chronic fatigue, lethargy,
- Neural diseases and imbalance
- Tinnitus, ringing of the ears, blocked sinuses (also links to the liver)
- Mood swings, weight gain, temperature deregulation e.g. hot flushes, non-distinctive overall pain
- Poor sleep patterns
- Mental Health- Depression, Anxiety, Melancholy, Suicidal thoughts
- A sense of lack of purpose and meaning in life

24.

CROWN CHAKRA – SAHASRARA
"Thousand Petals"

"My true happiness unfolds like a lotus flower to the light, one petal at a time"

Overview-
Sahasrara, the most common Sanskrit name for the Crown chakra, means 'thousand-petal-ed. This energy centre controls our connection to spirit and our sense of universal consciousness, wisdom, unity and self-knowledge.

If the Crown Chakra was nature itself, it would be all of the elements, it would be the soil, the rain and water, the Air, the Sun and the Moon, and it is the whole encompassing essence of all that is. It is the space of what holds all as one, it is the universal field of consciousness.

It is our connection to the universal field, to Source, the Devine to God, however we wish to name it for our own understanding. It is the meeting point, and our connection to Mother Earth and Father Sky, the essence that has created us and sustains us, a point of singularity.

Crudely, I see us as the adapter that brings two electric cables together, and holds them in place, allowing this communication and flow, a connection point to upload and download!

The chakra is violet and white, the far side of the visible light spectrum. Merging the whole, encompassing the white light that is through every colour that we see, for colour is a perception of our minds.

The symbol of the circle, which is in every chakra, represents infinity, our energy, our life force. Our essence is a cycle, death and rebirth physically, and emotionally as transformation. We are a continuation of our Soul and Spirit in many forms, gathering experiences, learning and wisdom of each cycle, whether these are days, months, years and lifetimes - *as energy cannot be destroyed simply transformed!*

Our essence is the same as water, it holds the memory of everything it has been in contact with, through every lifetime and existence, our soul lineage and through our generations of ancestors, our Earth lineage carried through us from the beginning of humanity.

It is with enlightenment and awareness that we are able to heal these cycles and patterns, the unfolding of each petal, is a moment to open, release and connect. The radiant lotus flower has risen up from deep murky water, remaining pure, yet still holds its roots to where it has grown from, providing part of its life sustenance and holding its place, to not be swept away.

It holds boundaries and the discernment of what is pure, filtering and only absorbing what it needs to its highest good, even in the darkest of surroundings.

We are most similar, from where we have grown from and through life's challenges and traumas. We do not try to ignore and disconnect from, we rise and grow, fully accepting our past, shadows and the pathway that has brought us to the present moment. Yet with awareness and enlightenment, we hold the power of discernment, we create our healthy boundaries and focus on what serves and nurtures us, and recognise what does not.

The greater the acceptance of who we are, the greater the connection to our purest essence, our purpose and joy, our place in the world and what we are here for – a gentle opening spiral, a lotus, one petal at a time.

"I am connected as one, to the life force and to all that supports and sustains the health of my mind, body and soul"

The Cycle of Nature and development — 20-27 years, we are an individual fully interacting with the world, with questions such as, *"why am I here, what is my purpose?"*

The Sanskrit mantra sound Sohum, meaning "I am He/She/That". In Vedic philosophy, it is the process of identifying oneself.

The bringing together of the knowledge and understanding of the essence of the soul, spirit and the universe as one, the recalling of all of our lifetimes, gifts and wisdom, to our present being and moments.

"I serve in a way that serves my joy and contentment"
"My presence in this world is a gift"

Mental - Emotional –Physical- the Crown chakra relates and influences the higher brain functions of the cerebral cortex, the limbic system, and links to the pituitary gland of the endocrine system

Collectively, our cerebral cortex is responsible for the higher-level processes of the human brain, including language, memory, reasoning, thought, learning, decision-making, emotion, intelligence and personality.

The limbic system, the seat of the autonomic nervous system, our subconscious, is involved in our behavioural and emotional responses. Especially when it comes to behaviours we need for survival, such as feeding, reproduction, caring for our young and the fight or flight responses.

The crown is the space between our primal subconscious needs to survive and our conscious choice to thrive. This filtration of our higher consciousness holds moments of meta-consciousness, an objectivity of self-reflection and observation, the pause of the cycle that enables us to have conscious thoughts. Of higher frequencies, such as compassion, empathy and peace, they are pivotal moments to break free of old patterns and cycles, to realign with what serves us to our highest and greatest good.

It is the filter of choice and discernment; of what are necessary survival actions, and those that are not, those that have been ingrained as subconscious belief systems and to have the empowerment of choice, to thrive, to experience our joy, love and peace – our purpose.

The crown links and influences every chakra, similar to an infrastructure of integral cogs. How the wheels of thought and perception, (the brow and crown) influence the downward chain of the cogs, through the efferent neurons, and how the lower cogs/chakras, feed back to the brow and crown via the afferent neurons.

It is the flow and balances of these chain reactions that create homeostasis of our mind and body in a state of wholeness. From the mental to the physical, our emotions are the energetic flow between the two, the driving force that determines lubrication, fluidity and efficiency of each cog and chakra system.

The heart is the breathing space, the stillness to re-evaluate, to let go of emotional patterns that block our flow and joy, and to align with what does; like the clutch returning to neutral, to decide which gear is optimum at that moment.

Flowing through the heart, our blood the carrier of the emotions from our sacral chakra, is a checking point. With the element of air, it has the ability to shift one's thought processes, patterns and cycles, when in coherence with the mind, and our higher state of consciousness – unconditional LOVE, is our pure true essence of being.

The transitioning of our brain waves follow a similar pattern influenced by both internal and external stimuli, ranging from Alpha–Beta –Theta-Delta-Gamma.

Cerebrospinal Fluid - The chakra includes the Choroid plexus, which are a network of blood vessels in each ventricle of the brain, producing the cerebrospinal fluid, throughout the central nervous system, our life force, it also bathes the pineal gland, as the gland is outside of the blood brain barrier.

Boundaries- Established energetic boundaries from thought and consciousness, with awareness of our place and connection within the world, and a healthy objectivity and connection, in compassion and empathy.

The Crown chakra relates to the physical boundaries of the skin and the blood brain barrier.

Balance and optimum flow –

Imbalance –closed and restricted – you feel isolated and easily fall into depression – find it difficult to meditate or pray and to quieten the mind. A sense of feeling uninspired in life, and overly concerned with the material life.

Too open – no boundaries,
- Find it challenging to integrate spiritual beliefs; spirituality becomes an addiction with possible separation and dissociation from the physical body. Eating poorly, with lack of exercise etc.
- Highly empathetic, connected to others emotions and energy field, take on others emotions as their own and often unable to distinguish the difference. May find themselves in a dynamic of Empath/Narcissist relationships.
- Often easily manipulated by others emotions and feel unable to put one's own needs and desires first – unable to see a way out of a situation
- Common to have moments of complete overwhelm, stress and anxiety, especially if not grounded fully in your body.

Physical Imbalance –
- Sensitive to pollution in the environment, including EMF (Electro Magnetic Frequencies)
- Headaches, Migraines
- Endocrine and hormone related illnesses
- Neurodegenerative diseases – Motor Neuron Diseases- Parkinsons, Alzheimer's
- Skin disorders
- Brain Fog, loss of clarity and focus
- Chronic fatigue and pain
- Neural diversity

"My true happiness unfolds like a lotus flower to the light, one petal at a time"

"The more you kick and scream, bite, scratch and try to run away, the darker the skies will get. You cannot run away from your pain and you cannot outrun the storm. By embracing your pain and bringing it within to heal, you empower your own growth. Accept what is, what was, and what is yet to come. This is the path to inner peace."

LJ Vanier

The crown chakra is focused to raise our vibration and frequency and to heal and return us to a state of wholeness, a connection to all that is, to recognise the illusion of separation and fear.

Like the petals opening one at a time, we heal through releasing lower vibrations of our energetic essence. As the light flows through our connection to Source, it cleanses, alchemises and transforms the challenging energies and shadows; the emotional imprints such as fear, guilt and shame, freeing and liberating ourselves, to resonate in states of gratitude, love, joy and inner peace.

The key is to set intentions of working through your healing gracefully and with ease, rather than avoidance, which eventually creates an opening of a dam effect. Or an impatience to get it done, the deluge becomes an overwhelm of trauma to process. For if we just seek the shadows, only the shadows will be seen!

I went down this path, my impatience *"to just get it done!"* I realised, always seek the light, the shadows will be revealed in time; at least this way, you are going in the right direction – up!

Remember we are infinite beings in a finite moment, we have layers upon layers to heal, and it is not a rush to get to the end, for who knows where the end is!

Allow thoughts to flow with objectivity and awareness, to come and go with ease and grace, hold space for you in self-care and fill these moments of healing with joy, love and acceptance of the wonderful unique miracle that you are.

Death is an illusion, life is a Dream
And we are the creator of our own imagination
The present moment is the only moment available to us and is the doorway to all moments

LJ Vanier

25.

THE BRIDGE OF CONNECTION

The image of reflection is captured through the perception of the mind

The sixth chakra is located in the centre of the forehead and is called Ajna, the Sanskrit translation "to command", "to perceive" or "beyond wisdom".

It is directly related to the senses of sight and hearing, and is said to provide an insight, an inner vision and enlightenment beyond the physical eye, transcending from the material world that we see or believe to see, to not only see, but to understand the inner and outer worlds. When stimulated, both hemispheres of the brain work together and help us transcend dualistic thinking.

The brow chakra is closely linked with the throat and crown chakras, they are physically close to one another representing and regulating our communication and understanding with the world. Coherence and a balanced flow of these three chakras are imperative for us to function and navigate within this world.

The throat chakra influences the mouth and jaw up to the ears, supported and separated by the sphenoid bone, which form the roof palate of our mouth and part of the ear canal. Whilst the brow has more links with the face, eyes, nose and forehead, they both influence the neck and the back of the head, the occiput, which supports the occipital lobe of the cerebrum, relating to the crown chakra.

The carotid nerve plexus that runs alongside the carotid artery of the neck highlights this connection of the throat and brow, as the nerve forms connections with the superior cervical ganglion, to the superior laryngeal nerve, travelling inferiorly and wrapping around the superior thyroid artery.

The carotid plexus fibres run with the carotid arteries and provide sympathetic innervation to the head, including supply to the dilator muscles of the iris; lacrimal glands, which are our tear glands maintaining the ocular surface; and the salivary glands. The levator palpebrae; a small muscle of the superior orbit, that elevates and retracts the upper eyelid; and the erector pili muscles, which are the tiny muscles that attaches to the base of a hair follicle at one end, and to the dermal tissue that cause our hairs to stand up.

Therefore, any impingements of the neck, throat and thyroid, physically and or emotionally, we can see how they could cause restriction to our brow chakra and our senses especially the eyes and ears. If our throat chakra is out of balance, unable to speak one's truth with heart felt kindness, compassion and integrity, due to an overpowering of fear within the solar plexus blocking the emotional flow of the sacral chakra and expression of our hearts. The centre of perception, our awareness, is also inhibited and equally any blockages of the brow would cause restrictions of the throat. We cannot speak our truth unless we are able to truly see, hear and feel our truth!

Often restrictions in the neck and head are due to not being able to see from a different perspective.

"A miracle is a shift of perspective"

Our seat of perception

Our brow chakra is also known as the third eye which governs how we see the world and how we process all that we experience in the world. Through this processing, all that we see on the outside is an expression of what we believe on the inside.

Therefore, a Miracle is a shift of perception, to dream, to visualise and to manifest through connection of oneness of the unified energy field of the Universe.

It is most interesting that this chakra is also known as the third eye, especially when we look within the structure of the brain and the organs involved namely the thalamus, pineal gland and the basal ganglia and their intricate functions, as they actually resemble the shape of an eye.

Before I go into more detail of these said structures, I had to include the exciting coincidence of the Egyptian Eye of Horus, the '*all seeing eye*' in the ancient Egyptian belief system. Legends have said that Horus was born as an "immaculate conception" from the virgin Goddess Isis and Osiris the Egyptian God, who was divided into fourteen pieces following a battle with his evil brother Set (Horus's Uncle).

Story is told that only thirteen pieces of Osiris were found and recovered, which were woven back together to enable him to pass to the Underworld. Horus was born through magick of Isis without the fourteenth piece, Osiris's penis, which was eaten by a fish within the River Nile!

It is thought that some of these pieces represent our senses, the five of sight, hearing, touch, taste and smell, the sixth of inner wisdom and knowing with the ability to connect to our truth, our perception derived from discernment, thus a higher perspective. A connection to our higher spiritual self, a step towards embodied enlightenment, of greater mind and heart consciousness.

The fourteen pieces I believe represent the fourteen cranial nerves, thought to be only been twelve pairs. The overlooked nerves X111 and XIV relate to our ears, sense of smell, our sinuses, our ability to discern, the Cerebrospinal Fluid, and the Luteinising Hormone, also known as the Gonadotropin-Releasing-Hormone, thus our sex drive and activity.

For me this is showing us the keys to access our connection to our creator, to God, to Source, through consensual loving acts of pleasure and sex. Within a state of connection, trust and surrender, free from fear and ill intent, rebirths this sacred reunion of the masculine and feminine.

The Eye of Horus-

There are two eyes, the left - *the eye of Ra*; and the right, *the eye of Horus*, both with different meanings and representation, which vary in interpretation, believed to be reunited by Thoth through peace.

The legend behind the Eyes of Horus is one of regeneration and healing, promoting a more positive symbolism that promises Divine intervention and protection from the gods.

In contrast, the Eye of Ra, the embodiment of the Sun God's daughters, most likely Sekhmet (The Goddess of Death and Rebirth), has a legend of hate and destruction; therefore, it's a symbol of protection borne of power, fury, and violence. *Personally, I see her as the Fire Goddess empowered by love that takes no shit!*

This could be also be inferred as our Higher Self, our Soul of pure love and light and our Ego of fear and shadows. How both voices merge at the centre of our brain, the pineal gland! It is our choice, our free will to hold a balance and awareness of both to act accordingly.

To be the balance of our sympathetic and parasympathetic nervous systems, to find a homeostasis and coherence of the body, the body's inner peace - to know when to act through self-love as protection rather than fear, and the ability to consciously discern what is fear and what is love.

Other interpretations say the left eye, the eye of Horus also represents the moon, the feminine/Yin energy, exploring creativity, sexuality, human nature and our emotions, intuition and magick, a symbol of healing powers and protection.

In contrast the right eye, the Eye of Ra represents the sun, the masculine energy Yang energy, that explores reason, mathematics, logic, science and language; a symbol of good luck and creative action. It is interesting how both sides embody both masculine and feminine, Horus masculine represents and holds the feminine, the Moon; and the eye of Ra-Sekhmet the "dark" feminine embodies the masculine the Sun; the yin-yang and dance of life in balance, equality and equilibrium.

Developed research has moved away from the thought that we are more dominant in one side of the brain than the other; however, acknowledge the predominant functions of both.

The left hemisphere of the brain controls the muscles on the right side; it processes information analytically and sequentially. Processing details and patterns to form the whole picture to have a broader perspective and create order and strategies. Responsible for verbal and language for both right and left handed people, however, less for left handed.

The right hemisphere of the brain controls the muscles on the left side of the body; it processes information intuitively through visual and is responsible for attention. Interesting, as we all seek eye contact from others, to know we have their attention, the saying the "eyes glazed over" to have lost someone's interest. I know I ask for my children's eye contact to hope I have their attention, and ensure I make eye contact when listening to others, especially with my clients.

The right side in opposite to the left, processes from the whole picture to details, so we can see how the two flow together, bringing pieces of input forming the whole, and then dividing back out for action, spanning in and out of the micro and macro vision, to create a balanced perspective.

The right side functions include spatial perception, which is the ability to recognise an object's physical location as well as the physical relationships between objects. To be able to perceive and visually understand outside spatial information such as features, properties, measurement, shapes, position and motion.

It also relates to our own relationship within our environment and the orientation of one's body, despite distracting information, this could be expanded to how we see our place in this world, our purpose. The right hemisphere is responsible for seeing possibilities in situations, to see the whole picture and focus on the positive from the negative, a characteristic most needed to manifest what we wish to see and be, it also brings hope and empowerment to the individual.

The Duality of Oneness -

For me this brings wholeness and balance when elements of duality, mirror images join together, becoming one. Structurally, the two hemispheres of the brain joined together by the two thalami part of diencephalon, a hidden section of the brain, which is surrounded by the 3rd ventricle. All communicating with one another, via the interthalamic adhesion and the pineal gland, which is located within the epithalamus, both having great similarities to the pupil of the eyes of Horus.

Interestingly, the pons and the medulla of the central nervous system also look like an eagle. Horus the Egyptian eagle-headed god, is known for his insight and psychic awareness, with the ability to travel between the worlds. The eagle is one of the highest flying animals connecting both the Sky and Earth, benefitting from a high perspective for an Earth born animal, and was revered to have the closest connection to the Gods.

The only bird that dares to peck an eagle is the crow. The crow sits on the eagles back and bites his neck. The eagle does not respond, nor fight with the crow; it does not spend time or energy on the crow, instead, he just opens its wings and begins to rise higher in the heavens.

This feels most profound to me, it is not about wasting our energy with fight or fear against situations, which may feel or perceived to be, trying to bring us down, instead to resolve we need to ascend and raise our frequency.

26.

THE EYES TELL IT ALL

Tears are a safety valve of the heart when too much pressure is laid upon it.
Dale E. Turner, Different Seasons

I believe the reason why we cry, is to release the emotions through the water, the element of the sacral, as it rises up within our body, gathering the emotions stored within our abdominal stomach area, and our heart, for acceptance and acknowledgement. Continuing the rise up through our throat, the guard and governor of what we allow in and out, our boundary keeper, and then finally releasing out through our eyes.

Crying is a deep process for us to express, understand and see our emotions for what they are, be they of love, joy and deep gratitude or of fear, hurt, anger, shame and guilt.

For those that have watched a movie with others that has made you want to cry, yet do not wish to appear "soft" in front of others, that you hold back, feeling the lump in one's throat, not allowing ourselves to truly embrace and release our emotions.

This process of crying highlights how all the chakras are interlaced, and when we allow ourselves to breathe and channel these emotions in a safe supportive way, we create a therapeutic space of objective awareness. To allow the process of release without the reattachment of the emotion to draw one back in to the drama, cleansing the mind and body as whole. I like to imagine that our emotions are coming to the surface are like clouds in the sky, we watch with a quiet awareness with no attempt to control, we simply let them come and then let them go.

Conscious breathing techniques are fundamental in supporting our mind and body to release, as they form the bridge of our peripheral nervous system. Whilst activating the somatic nervous system through conscious movement, we tap and flow into the autonomic nervous system that naturally heals and repairs our bodies seeking balance. As we breathe we are activating our heart chakra to open and to form our mind and heart coherence, holding a space to accept and acknowledge our emotions, as we visualise our breath into our sacrum and hips, stomach and heart, and release as we breathe out through our throat and mouth.

> *The heart is frozen... and the tears are the beginning of its melting.*
> Bhagwan Shree Rajneesh, Osho,

Personally, one profound experience of consciously blocking my emotions was at the funeral of my grandmother. In fact, now as I write this the tears come to my eyes, bringing to the surface emotions that I believed I had already processed and released. I can remember adamantly not wanting to cry and "lose" control at the service, I had a strange perception that I had to keep strong and hold my grief and tears within, which I managed to suppress.

However, days later when I wanted to cry, to grieve about the loss of my Nana (the last of my grandparents), I could not, which could only be described as a deep block within the subconscious. This deep suppression of highly charged emotions of grief transpired soon after, and for many months into a new sense of self-loathing fuelled by a torrent of other emotions of guilt, hurt, separation.

I had this itch under my skin on my arms and wrists that I just wanted to scratch, becoming an act of self-harming, fortunately just with my nails, I can only imagine it was a voice of self-love that held me back from completely falling into this black hole of self-attack and separation.

> *Un-cried tears have a way of filling the well of sadness even more deeply.*
> Robert J. Grover, Professor Emeritus, Susan G. Fowler,

From what I understand now, this powerful triggered emotional state that released these emotions would have been released naturally through my throat chakra as tears and sobbing. Yet being closed and fearful of expression, these emotions were trapped within my central nervous system with no exit, like free radicals causing chaos, stress, inflammation and heat within.

This was also a time of my life when I was in an unhappy controlling narcissist relationship, yet seemed unable to acknowledge, to accept and see my truth and voice that it was not serving me joy or purpose.

I share this personal experience in a space of vulnerable self-love and acceptance to hopefully be the light for others to recognise we all at some point go through challenges. We are not alone in this roller-coaster of life, yet with a quiet centred awareness of self, we can navigate through these expansions and constrictions with more integrity and truth, for ourselves and our relationships.

What I have learnt also, is that grief connects with grief, once you allow it to move through you, all other layers of grief begin to release like a wave, a catalyst to clear the sorrow and pain that blocks our love and joy. When you feel the grief moving through you, the ache in your heart, breathe deeper into your heart and allow this movement to flow, trust this process and your body. I often do the *cat-cow* pose to support this process – to allow whatever noises I need to let go. We can often feel washed out, like the ocean is taking us, however, if connected, grounded embodied, through breath and awareness, you will feel more centred, and less fearful.

> *"The eyes are the mirror of the soul and reflect everything that seems to be hidden; and like a mirror, they also reflect the person looking into them."*

When we converse with others we subconsciously seek eye contact, when we look into each other's eyes we connect physically and energetically. If we wish to, we are able to dive deeper on an emotional and spiritual level with one another through this connection.

Firstly, an exercise of looking in the mirror at yourself and see what you see. Listen to your thoughts and perception of self; are they negative or positive, are they of love or are they of fear and disapproval and disconnection to self?

Take note on how you feel about yourself and the scale of love and acceptance you have for this wonderful miracle looking back at you. Find a kind word for that being in front of you, start to see or even set the intention to see the beauty within YOU!

For my life that I can recall, has been looking at my reflection, sabotaging her for not being good enough, too fat, boobs, thighs, butt not right, etc.; only a small part of me did I accept as OK and even then I did not want to be too boastful, to seem arrogant! I would never have dreamt of saying these hateful words to anyone else, so why do I think it is ok to say them to myself?

Even when younger, beautiful and slim, I still had this negative perception of myself, I look back at photos of myself and see a beautiful woman, with a sense of grief of the loss of the joy I could have had if I had accepted myself then. my drive to change and shift to a more loving caring narrative and perception of myself in every conscious moment.

If this resonates with you, I implore you to be willing and set the intention to start loving and accepting yourself more on all levels, physically, emotionally and spiritually. To finally unleash the shackles and enjoy being the wonderful miracle that you are, in a subconscious way you already are, as you are reading this right now! Our highest self, our soul is always trying to guide us to grow and experience more joy, which gets even more exciting when we consciously connect and surrender to this wisdom and guidance!

The eyes will lead us to the depth of the person, their soul and their truth, when we open our senses of perception.

The eyes in Traditional Chinese Medicine link to the liver's health. The liver represents our relationship with our deep inner self, it stores anger, and deeper still, betrayal and bitterness. It has the ability to eliminate toxicity and regenerate, and it is the wood element, the fuel to the fire, connecting the liver and heart.

Suppressing these deep emotions is like a fire with barely any oxygen, it cinders generating a deep heat burning down and suffocation of the body and spirit. This prolonged heat in the body creates inflammation and dehydration, hence, any eye issues, for example, dry eyes may relate to unresolved anger and hurt.

I remember as a child looking at someone's eyes and somehow knowing that their liver was not healthy. This I can only explain as an inner wisdom, as I was not taught this at that time.

When in contact with others, looking into their eyes, do they seem distant, distracted, avoiding contact, with a film coating, seem dimmed and glazed? Has the fire of that person burned out, are they carrying too much rage, to mask the hurt, or do their eyes shine brightly with energy and a sparkle, with an enthusiasm and connection with you?

We get a sense of a person, when we hold space to be fully present with them, not just listening to their words, yet also the tone of their words, which is determined by the health and function of our Vagus nerve. Are they really meaning what they say, are they really ok, do they actually believe in what they are saying, or are they reciting what they have been told as their truth? Is there spice and elevation in their tone, or is it more mono-tone and joyless, do they have passion, are their eyes open and wide with enthusiasm, a softness holding good intentions, or are they hard and piercing?

Little note, when we tell the truth we look upwards to recall our memory, when we are being liberal with the truth we look down.

Without knowing, we instinctively look to people's eyes to read and understand that person. If meeting someone for the first time, we are subconsciously questioning whether we are safe, are they similar to me, are they part of my tribe, and am I accepted? A genuine smile will often quieten our primitive mind and rest more in their company.

This is why masks that became the common thing during covid19, actually increased anxiety even more so. In addition to the fear of being too near, something that is the complete opposite of our basic needs as a human, the need for contact and touch, which actually reduces our stress levels and improves our immunity!

27

TRUSTING OUR LAYERS OF INSIGHT – OUR SIXTH SENSE

We are also subconsciously reading each other's energetic fields from our heart and gut, as they too, are listening and connecting to form a perception. Our hearts magnetic field extends 3 feet, approximately, roughly an arm's length and the same for the other person, meaning we can feel each other's energy with our hearts 6 feet away, the good old saying keeping one at arm's length has meaning here!

Our energy fields intertwine as we become closer emotionally and physically, highlighting the imperative need for healthy boundaries especially if you are an "Empath" an energetic sponge, potentially taking on others issues. Interestingly, the liver also acts a sponge, so we can absorb others negativity and toxicity unconsciously!

When we wish to understand, we predominantly seek with our eyes, to be able to see our truth externally. I often see people with a deep furrowed brow between the eyes, as they are intensely trying to read and understand life from external stimuli, that truth can only be understood if it can be seen as such.

However, we have multiply layers and senses to connect to, for our real truth to be born we must seek within ourselves, our in-sight.

Our insight is built upon a formation, a hub of senses, our smell, our hearing, our skin and touch, our taste, our hearts, our gut instinct and the whispers of our inner knowing if we are quiet and still enough to listen.

Our sense of smell goes directly to the cerebrum and into our Autonomic Nervous System (ANS) via the Olfactory nerve, aka Cranial Nerve I, bypassing the thalamus, our seat of perception and conscious thought. It creates an instinctive response. The saying "something doesn't smell right, or I smell BS" is our instinctive inner knowing, telling us something is wrong and does not resonate with us, with our truth. We can also smell through taste connecting to the olfactory nerve, the saying "something to chew on", means to think about something before making a decision.

The direct relationship from our sense of smell and taste feeding directly to our cerebrum, highlights why aromatherapy oils and scents are great for getting into our ANS to stimulate a response of calm or activity depending on what we desire.

When we soften the importance of what we see and gently trust how we feel, connecting to the wisdom of the body centres, we create a more rounded vision and understanding. Sometimes we may not know how or why, yet we come to a peaceful acceptance that not everything has to be understood to be accepted.

Upon this, we give ourselves the permission to trust ourselves more and to tap into our inner magick, power and wisdom. With this leap of faith we allow the process of surrender, realising our perception of control and allow the magick to flow. The more we trust, the more it flows.

You Do Not Need to Understand to Accept!

This came up for me when I was meditating once. I was trying to understand the expanse of the Universe, our souls, our spirits, our life, previous lives, and I was basically told you do not need to understand to accept! Well, that told me…ha!

I was then shown as to how we learn and grow, from our early days and foundation years our eyes and stimuli, connect to the thalamus where 98% of our perception is formed; imprinting memories into our limbic system, our emotional centre, with the ultimate goal to find consistency, control and coherence of all stimuli. The brain, limbic, cerebral and cerebrum hold these patterns and associations to bring order, otherwise, we would be overwhelmed and would have to learn the same thing every day and would not progress.

To understand things the brain has to compartmentalise, a separation and labelling, forging a pattern and belief to navigate our day to day life. However, to understand that the Universe and all that it encompasses is ONE, all is an extension from the same source, therefore, we are unable to separate, meaning the human brain is unable to compute the expanse of the Universe, it blows our mind!

When Love is Present Fear is a Stranger!

However, our hearts have a greater frequency than our minds, 5000 times, and have the ability to connect to the oneness of the universe. With the same neurons of conscious processing found in our minds, our hearts hold this potential of inner knowing and acceptance to be seen and felt through the lens of love. It is with the opening and expansion of the heart to receive this wisdom, and the coherence of mind that enables us to walk our paths more in trust, love and acceptance.

What hinders and blocks this trust are the patterns, beliefs and perceptions that we have formed in our early years, which can play out for us as adults if unaware and unattended. Fear experienced becomes recorded in the amygdala of the limbic system and is triggered whenever the similar vibrations of events are experienced. Which helps us understand, our contracted responses whether defensive or aggressive to people and situations. It could be a smell, a word, a tone, a look, a feeling of unworthiness, of being unheard, a feeling of being unsafe or unsupported that brings up these old unhealed emotions and wounds.

Often the moments of darkness and shadows are the golden nuggets of healing, for there to be shadow, so there must also be light!

However, when we are aware that this event and trigger is there to unearth what no longer serves us purpose or joy, we begin to transform to see it as a gift to heal rather than the old negative narrative we tell ourselves; the self-sabotage, no one listens, no one loves me! We become more conscious, that the trigger, the person, the event, is an energetic mirror holding up for you to see what you need to shift and release, to return to your true pure essence, your expansive light and love.

When we accept we are beings of energy, we see each moment as a reflection to expand within

Don't get me wrong, the process of healing and transformation isn't all fairy tales and magic, with a wave of a wand and Cinderella is a Princess. It hurts, it sucks and it's raw as we reconnect to our pain, our hidden trauma which we have covered up in shadows and disassociation. However, the greater consciousness held the less vortices of emotional pain is felt.

"Triggered moments of the Present are windows of healing of the Past To create gateways for our Future"

Pain follows the same neural pathways as the emotion of loneliness and separation, and when we fragment ourselves, closing ourselves and toning down the emotional pain, in a way to survive the situation, we shut down and compromise the cells, the tissues and the organs relevant to these emotions. Hence pain and dis-ease are our bodies calling to us for attention, for reconnection and healing.

Once we make the connection to the disconnection consciously via our neural pathways, in a safe, supported space, we permit the body to release these trapped layered emotions, which are suffocating our cells. Enabling them to bring light and life back to them, we begin the journey of returning to a state of wholeness, coherence and health.

If you believe you have deep trauma work to process, it is vital to establish a strong supportive network, including professional help.

When we have this miracle in our shift of perception, we then allow the process of healing, to know this is not your truth, this is not what you are destined for. We begin to navigate from the state of awareness to acceptance, the healing energy and cutting cords, through forgiveness and later the release. The letting go and freeing ourselves, to create our own paths, not to walk the paths others, ancestors and society have set for us.

This may take some time depending on the depth of the wounds and trauma, so hold compassion and love for yourself as you do.

If it is your inner child seeking love, safety and acceptance, then nurture and self-parent yourself, with what you were seeking as a child, gift them to yourself. For instance, if you were not heard, listen to your inner child, hold space for them; if they needed to feel safe, hold them like you would a child, reassure them they are safe now, *"I have you"*, whatever words you needed to hear then, speak them now.

Inner child healing is triggered deeply when you have children of you own, or are trying to have a family. It is like we have these mirrors held back at us to see, to make the choice to change these patterns that have run through our ancestral lineage, for us to act as the lineage breaker to shift humanity into the light.

Our parents consciously or unconsciously will layer their inner thoughts and beliefs onto us, even when they speak differently. As children, we are reading every move, every energetic vibe. These become our patterns to follow, to be part of the tribe, to be accepted. Therefore, the best parents we can be, if a parent or a role model for others, is to be it, to be what we want to see, that is our power, that is how we make a difference!

Please see the VOICE podcast if you would like to understand this more
   https://www.podbean.com/media/share/pb-c25v7-1305aa6

Thanks Gran!

Then we have the layers that are not even of our lifetime. Our DNA not only carries down our genetic makeup, how we look, our health, it also hands down the unprocessed emotions and trauma, held within the energetic cellular matrix of our ancestors, especially the matriarchal lineage. It is called imprinting, which although cannot be proven, would go back to the beginning of humanity. Let's face it, humanity has seen its fair amount of trauma, inhumane acts, war, deceit betrayal and hurt!

We will have beliefs, thought processes and emotional responses that actually have no tangible connection to our life's experiences. When we self-reflect deeply; listening to our bodies responses we may have no correlation to this visceral trigger. These imprinted beliefs, emotions and trauma, lay in our subconscious mind and the cells of our body underneath the radar of our conscious mind.

This may account for reasons of congenital health issues, as the emotions stored in their energetic framework, visceral organs and blood continues through to us.

Our mitochondria may well be the answer, as individual's mitochondrial genome is entirely derived from the mother because sperm contain relatively few mitochondria, and these are degraded after fertilisation. It follows that mitochondrial inheritance is essentially maternal inheritance. Studies are exploring how imprinted emotional trauma is genetically passed through our maternal ancestral lineage and the carriers may well be the mitochondrial genome, chromosomes.

Therefore, our health and energy levels are reliant on the health of our mitochondria within every of the trillion of cells. Certain mental and physical symptoms may be a latent trauma imprinting through our generations, bypassing our conscious and subconscious, and held within the unconscious mind and our energetics. To finally be acknowledge and released, to allow the pattern to break for ourselves, for our children and their children to come.

Update - Studies are actually now showing that 50 generations of trauma is held within the Mitochondria – this is huge as it validates what I see when healing others – love it when Science catches up!

Drawing a line in the sand – Becoming the Pattern Breaker -

Great I hear you say, thanks Gran! However, we have the power to change the expression of our DNA, we can transform our epigenome through conscious choices. As stress can change and damage the DNA in the mitochondria within the cells, positivity can also heal, through the power of love, joy, inner peace and contentment, the wonderful hormone of oxytocin aka "the love hormone" is imperative to this.

"I Choose Joy - I Choose Love - I Choose Peace"
"I am Worthy of Love "I am Worthy of Joy "I am Worthy of Peace"
"I am Love – I am Joy – I am Peace"

Visualisation and meditation activates our internal command centre, our third eye, by choice we can through neuroendocrine and neural plasticity, create new pathways and tracks of thought, to lead us to more joy, love and inner peace and contentment.

Once we become conscious and objective to our emotions, as we detach from our self-identity to them, we begin to allow ourselves to unmask and process this ancestral trauma, and quite possibly our Soul Lineage, karma too.

Know Thyself

28.

PARADOX – DUALITY AS ONE – BALANCE

"the paradox is one of our most valuable spiritual possessions…only the paradox comes anywhere near the comprehending the fullness of life"
                                                                    Carl Jung

Our third eye represented with the two lotus petals forming a circle becoming one with a downward triangle signifies, when open, centred and grounded. It allows us to see from a higher perspective, to see all aspects, a 360degree observation, to have a balanced outlook on one's experiences, to enable us to observe ourselves free from the vortex and the triggered state of emotions.

We begin to understand and accept that our opposites and our paradoxes need to exist for the other to exist. To navigate and dance gracefully between them to achieve balance

In the words of Brené Brown Atlas of the Heart; *"a paradox is the appearance of contradiction between the two related components"*

For instance, without light, we would not see the spectrum of colour, shadows and depth, without shadows; we would not have a presence; without darkness we would not see the light of the stars; without our shadows and pain, we would not understand nor appreciate our light and joy.

Survive and Thrive –Contraction & Expansion- Love-Fear – Soul-Ego
"Life becomes a graceful roller-coaster within awareness and acceptance"

Without the lows we would not have the highs, which for me, represents the line we see on heart monitors, the Heart Rate Variability (HRV). When healthy, it has a steady and consistent frequency, expansion and contraction, transitioning with ease between the sympathetic and parasympathetic nervous system. When we become stressed and/or stuck in a pattern of thought and beliefs, we restrict the shift and transcending of healing.

Relating this to our health, our body needs both paradoxes of our autonomic nervous system, we need the sympathetic to wake up in the morning to do our tasks and movement, we need it to be alive and functioning. Our parasympathetic nervous system is when our body heals in a resting state to restore, digest, nourish and procreate. Homeostasis is the balancing act of the two throughout our day and night, to repair our cells from oxidative stress, the free radicals released from the methylation and functioning of the trillion of cells within our bodies, which keeps us alive.

The sympathetic relates to our adrenal glands and our energy levels to function throughout the day, our early ancestors hunting and gathering their food. It is also our survival mode, a contracted response of fear, to function in moments that threaten our existence.

Yet remaining in this state mostly due to stress, which is fuelled by our subconscious and unconscious fears, we impede the transition to the parasympathetic system, which heals our mind and body, which blocks our experiences of joy, inner peace and contentment, to thrive.

Survival is to have our basic needs met, such as food, shelter and warmth, a sense of belonging and acceptance within our tribe, as to not be accepted would have meant rejection, thus survival was unlikely. To thrive, we need the reassurance and trust that all of our survival needs will be met, in both the physical and emotional, to know we are loved and accepted unconditionally, free from the fear of rejection.

Stress and trauma affect the structure and chemistry of the brain and can stunt its natural growth and maturation, highlighting how imperative our foundation years are for our growth as individuals.

When we rest comfortably in a peaceful state of love and acceptance, our brain releases a hormone called oxytocin that lowers blood pressure and cortisol levels. It increases pain thresholds, exerts an anxiolytic-like effect and stimulates various types of positive social interaction. In addition, it promotes growth and healing.

Fear helps us survive – yet resists us to thrive

To have the will to survive, we need to experience the comfort of love expanding into joy, settling to an inner peace and contentment; this is why food makes us happy, as one of our primitive needs have been met.

Eating disorders can be linked to whether our needs were met as an infant from being nurtured by the breast, snuggled in with skin to skin contact, to feel safe, loved and accepted as a child. If they were not we may find our need to cover up or substitute a sense of lacking with *"fake joy"* created by the bliss/happy hormone, dopamine. Dopamine is released when fat, sugar and salt are combined, especially high levels of sugar, which we find in processed foods.

Food manufacturers are quite savvy to this, they are not making foods that are healthy, they are making foods that you will "need" to buy again and again!

When we remain in our survival based nervous system from our primitive mind of fear, we are unable to experience joy and happiness in its purest form. We find ourselves looking for external stimuli to create our joy, yet joy in its purity and infinite flow, is found within.

Fear is an Illusion

Fear is an illusion unless in the life threatening present moment, fears are our primitive mind, also described as the ego, which is there to "protect" us. Fear is so deeply rooted in our systems, our patterns, beliefs and thought trails, that our behaviour feels "normal". Not only do we have our primitive mind of survival to contend with, we can have ancestral traumas and stress passed through our many generations. We also have social conditioning, the need of acceptance and belonging, which feeds back to our old survival needs.

Being mindful with awareness of self, our patterns and beliefs with self-reflection work, we are able to create a more balanced perspective, to shift from continuous reactive behaviour patterns to more composure and grace.

Fear is the energy of division; love is the energy of unity, of oneness, the bond of polarity.

Diversity is Acceptance held in the Presence and Expansion of Love
Division is Rejection Contracted in Fear

When we love, we also experience fear, our love for life, our love for others. This creates a paradox of love and fear, the fear of loss, the emotion of grief and separation. Yet love is an infinite bond that binds without restrictions, with freedom and expression, it is the energy that connects all through the physical, emotional and spiritual.

For when we recognise that we are all forms of energy, and when in a physical form, we are simply denser forms of that energy, and when we pass from this physical form, back to our energetic form, our connection continues. One is infinite, we are never truly separated in the energy of love.

With this knowing and connection in our hearts, we can hold peace an inner acceptance of our love, our grief, to know our energy of love binds to our loved ones in this ocean of energy; to be drawn upon, whenever we need that reassurance, to ask when we need that guidance and support, in ways we may not feel possible.

The Energy of Grief
Grief is an emotion to remind us of the sacred value of Life

Grief is not actually something to get over, or removed from our hearts and bodies, it is a matter of time, self-care and awareness, to hold a space of acceptance of such, to honour our pain and hurt.

The grief we feel is an extension of our love, to know we are never truly separated!

Love is the telephone wire reminding us of our connection through another level of communication!

In our hearts we hold the infinite bond of love, and within, we feel the aching tinge and contraction from the wave of grief.

Reminding us of our love for those that have passed from their physical and returning to their energetic imprint of pure essence.

This energetic imprint and memory lays within the cells of our hearts, a tapestry of our physical connection, our interaction and the precious time spent together, their existence alive in our hearts!

Grief is an emotional wave that will reconnect and trigger grief already held within our bodies. If we choose to restrict and suppress our raw emotion, we feel it in our throat, yet deeper still, in the delicate organ of the pancreas, unprocessed and undigested, down-tuning the sweetness of life.

Its energetic frequency wave, shakes up the emotional sediments to be acknowledged and "aired". Harnessing these moments to support us to come inward, to honour and respect our emotions, to allow our love entwined with grief to open our hearts to a new beautiful, powerful and vulnerable boundary, of expansion and expression.

Our open hearts and acceptance, allows our grief to flow whenever it needs to, kindly guiding and nurturing us inwards to a resting place of inner peace.

Love is Infinite

The Paradox of Light and Dark
Without night there would be no day, meeting in balance as dusk and dawn.

The colours of dusk and dawn are of pastel blues and pinks, the visible spectrum of light, from red to blue mixed with white light forms these colours. They are a balance of the two opposites with the spiritual light within, and when merged, they form indigo, which is the colour that represents the third eye and brow chakra. The relationship of the pineal gland also links to this, due to its function of night and day.

I have often wondered why these moments when observed in nature, feel so special and sacred. Mindful space of quiet contemplation, especially when graced with the splendour of colour, just before or after, as the sun rises and sets. These sacred moments are a wonderful time to sit in nature, to observe and be mindful of our thoughts and perceptions, to seek the higher perspective, balance and joy in life.

Self-reflective observation of what is not serving you joy or purpose, the key to this is to understand what we can actually control and that is our thoughts and our actions, the rest is up to the free will of the billions of other beings on this planet and the universe. Wisdom and inner peace comes from our acceptance of this!

Mindful observation of our thoughts and emotions is about creating space to observe what is playing out for us in our life. When life and the world feels challenging, ask yourself; how can I perceive this differently; how is this challenging me; how can I grow and heal from this; what intentions and actions am I able to make to feel empowered?

Is it a case of acceptance and surrender, am I able to release my perception of control and what positives am I able to get from this? Anything negative will have a positive as it would not exist, therefore, what positive can I take out of this and focus on, what would bring me into greater harmony within myself and my environment?

"Every Cloud has a Silver Lining"
"Where our Attention goes, our Energy Flows"

The positive would not exist without the negative. When we think of these polar opposites and our third eye is open and balanced, we can assess and self-reflect from an objective and higher perspective, elevated from the triggered responses and fearful patterns.

We can choose to find the positive that exists within the negative and focus our attention on this to create, as where our attention goes our energy flows! Therefore, to feel empowered and create the situations we wish to see, feel and be in this world, we need to shift and balance our perspective, our energy and our focus.

If we continue to keep ourselves in a negative outlook and response loop, focusing on what we do not wish to see in our lives and in the world itself, we as powerful energetic beings, begin to fuel and give energy to the negative. The complete opposite outcome we hope for, with our mind and body taking the toll!

It increases stress on the body as it remains within the heightened sympathetic nervous system, we increase a resistance in our body through fight and anger, generating friction, heat, dehydration and inflammation of the cells that links to pain, restricted range of movement of soft tissues and joints, illness and disease.

Through chronic and intense exposure to stress and trauma, caught within the negative cycle, we perceive ourselves as "stuck", our mobility of change is restricted. We feel helpless and hopeless, a complete disempowerment of self, which freezes the nervous system, unable to transition fluidly between the sympathetic and parasympathetic to find homeostasis.

I will say many times, *"A Miracle is the Shift of Perception"*! As our third eye is our command centre for the whole of our body via the small, yet mighty Pineal Gland. Our thoughts and emotions become energy-in-motion, the catalyst to our endocrine system and neuroendocrine pathways, our own cell communication network,

The brow and crown chakra are energy systems that interlink greatly, the Pineal Gland, our third eye, communicates with the Pituitary gland, the chief transmitter of the endocrine system, which is represented by the Crown chakra.

It is the perception and decision of the pineal gland and its energetic transmission to the pituitary gland; via the neuroendocrine system, the hypothalamus releases chemicals, our hormones to communicate to the cells, tissues and organs to respond accordingly.

Masculine – Feminine

Without one, neither would exist, neither is more important than the other. Whether you are male or female, we all have the energy of both and it is vital to balance for our health and wellbeing. It is a delicate dance between the two.

In Ayurveda, they have Nadis, which are energy channels throughout the body, similar to Chi in Traditional Chinese Medicine, the meridians which Acupuncture is based upon.

There are thousands of Nadis points, however, the three main channels are the Pingala, the Ida and the central channel, the Sushumna.

The Pingala, to mean tawny in Sanskrit, is the masculine represented as the sun, solar and yang energy, rising from our right side of the perineum (the space between the anus and scrotum in the male, or between the anus and the vulva in the female, our base chakra.

The Ida, to mean comfort in Sanskrit, is the feminine yin energy represented by the moon, rising from the left side of the perineum.

The two nadis channels criss-cross and overlap like a helix of DNA through the rising chakras, coming together at the third eye, linking the base and brow chakra, the perineum and the pineal gland. This connection merges our duality essence as one, the masculine and feminine, bringing a stable framework, enhancing and supporting each chakra to flow in coherence.

It is said that they carry the "prana", the air of life through them, and when open, balanced and flowing, it opens the Sushumna channel, the central line. Encompassing our spine and central nervous system, to allow the life force, the Kundalini, the Devine goddess, our Devine blueprint, our true essence to expand in all its beauty; creating the vital space for our sacred energy held within the sacrum, to rise up and flow into the crown chakra.

I see this as our physical representation of this energy, in denser form as the cerebrospinal fluid, the life force of our central nervous system.

It is this rising life force and energy that enables us to create a fusion of the Mother Earth to Father Sky; the physical body through the perineum to our pineal gland, connecting and communicating with the universal field of energy, to enlighten and to understand one's purpose and interaction within such.

This rising and ascending energy "uploading" through our physical, emotional, mental and spiritual energetic bodies, connects to the Source of life. For us to embody into our physical, we "download" through our minds and into our hearts to accept this consciousness into our being, within heart and mind coherence, creating a heart consciousness and space for our thoughts, perceptions and actions.

The Heart is the holding space in balance of Spirit and Soul, Mother Earth and Father Sky, to hold a space of creation that is unique.... You!

We are an expanded transmutation of an atom, with physical presence in the visible spectrum of light.

An atom is made of three parts, an electron that is negatively charged, a proton that is positively charged and a neuron that is neutral. I see the electron and proton as the masculine and feminine held within this neutral space.

The neuron, that is a blank canvas a space of pure potentiality, it can be whatever it chooses to expresses itself to be, as it draws upon the energy of both the sources of energy in balance, and how it interacts with the energy field that it is connected with.

In shamanism, we are the hollow bone of which the Devine-Source flows through us when we are in our true connection, when we are in a place of surrender and become a vessel for the Devine to fully express within us.

We are an expanded atom of both the physical, Mother Earth and Body Spirit in fusion with the Universe, Father Sky, the Devine, Our Soul, and our Highest Self. We are a hybrid of both, with the free will as to how we choose to interact with our sacred space within, and the universal space around us.

Our experiences are the transmutation of our energetic DNA – we can choose the expression of such once we honour and harness our inner power – our metaconsciousness, conscious and subconscious thoughts in constant "download" and "upload", within the universal field of consciousness.

Kundalini -Life Force

Kundalini is seen as a coiled spring, snake like, rising up, and represented by a triangle at the base, our sacrum (base of the spine); our body mirrors this in our genitals, as we have two triangles of the perineum forming a diamond shape.

The Kundalini is also represented as the Caduceus wand; a short staff entwined by two serpents, sometimes surmounted by wings, a symbol of rising up in balance to connect to the highest aspect of self. It is the staff carried by Hermes in Greek mythology and consequently by Hermes Trismegistus in Greco-Egyptian mythology, the combination of Hermes, Thoth and Archangel Raphael, the angel of healing.

This ancient wisdom is held across the globe, in Chinese, Tibetan Indian and European, all have similar records of these channels or energy, Qi, Prana, Kundalini. This wisdom held for thousands of years, have been layered into what we know now about our bodies. It has always been there, yet we have become disconnected from this wisdom, this magick and empowerment of self. It is now our time to reclaim our power and wisdom of our ancestors and dive deep within.

Throughout each day and night, our breath naturally cycles between dominance of one of the two energy channels, states of imbalance occur when one side or the other is chronically more restricted or closed than the other.

Alternate nasal breathing, Nadi-Shodhana-Pranyama which in Sanskrit translates as "channel" "purification" "life energy" "control"; is a wonderful technique to support the balance of the two hemispheres of the brain and the Ida and Pingala energy channels.

Whilst practicing the technique, I visually connect the perineum and the pineal gland, the centre of my mind, visualising white light flowing up either side of the spine and connecting the two.

Using gentle contraction of the intricate pelvic floor muscles with the breath, to act as a pump to assist the flow of the energy through the centre of the spine; visualising a cylinder of light. Acknowledging the curvature and releasing any blocks felt physically and energetically in one's mind. Moving the body supports this flow from the sacral to the crown.

It is important for our state of wholeness and health to accept the flow of our dualities, of the masculine and feminine energy in balance and equality.

The pure essence of the masculine is the protector, destroyer and creator; it gives presence and definition and is the energy of doing. The masculine energy establishes our boundaries with discernment, whereas the feminine is what gives these boundaries form, the feminine is the hidden energy that fills this space, equally holding the boundary.

The feminine is the maiden, mother and wise one that creates the holding space of community, connection, companionship, and co-creation.- as you shine, so do others! There is room for all to shine and radiate, and by uplifting one another you co-create a world that works for everyone

The masculine of our Sun is the solar energy – fire Yang, which is the energy of action and growth; and the feminine energy of our Moon, is the Sacral energy of water-Yin, the carrier of wisdom. The blueprint of all that is, the seed of fertility, it is also about space and the stillness within.

Interestingly, the mitochondria that is in the cells control centre, holds the light and life force within, and only derives from the mother. Our mitochondria are our blueprint upon which we are given life and grow from, which is also said for water.

29.

FINDING OUR BALANCE OF REST AND ACTION

On a cellular level, the masculine is the cell wall, the plasma membrane; the feminine is the interstitial fluid, both inside (intercellular ICF) and outside (Extracellular ECF) of the cell, found in blood plasma, lymph and cerebrospinal fluid.

The cellular wall is our first physical boundary holding structure, an outline of space, without such we would be mush. However, without the water to fill this space we would have no presence. With equal pressure called osmotic equilibrium, it creates a turgor (the force that pushes the plasma membrane of a cell against its cell wall). The essence of these energies gives presence and form of the cell. Multiplied by circa 70 trillion and we have our body.

Without this equilibrium and presence of both, the cell would not be able to function. It would be similar to a torrential rain storm, where all the earth banks of the rivers are washed away, becoming mud and sludge, gradually blocking any flow, life nor definition. Picture the beautiful banks of the streams and rivers supporting and creating a structure for the water to flow within, with serpentine grace and curvature, both providing life and sustenance for each other.

Any imbalance of the solutes concentration, the electrolytes in the water, which include sodium, potassium and calcium, the cell would either shrink or swell, affecting the turgor/pressure in the cell and the ECF found in our blood. Creating inflammation, pressure, toxicity, fatigue to eventually cell death. As we are ultimately a formation of trillion of cells, our health is our cell health. Key related symptoms of such, would be oedema, lymphatic issues, blood pressure, kidney health, and then anything else with "itis" in its name.

How we navigate our daily lives affects this flow of expansion and contraction, like our breath and cerebrospinal fluid, our heart beat.

Society for hundreds of years, have emphasised and solely focused on the sole energy of the masculine. A pressure of productivity, a forced drive against our natural rhythms, most likely attributed to the Industrial Revolution circa 1760, as man-made lighting enabled workforces to work beyond the hours of natural light. Working between 14-16 hours a day, 6 days a week, and later circa 1920's to 8-9 hour day shifts all year round.

Where previously farmers and hand trades people would have been regulated by daylight hours and the seasons, with longer hours in the Summer and less in the Winter. Living within the cycles of change and connection to Mother Earth, the seasons, the Sun and provided the nourishment for crops to grow. The moon when full, would have given extra light that was needed, especially at Harvest time, namely the Harvest Moon, which falls close to the Autumn Equinox.

Even with the longer hours, work was intermittent, allowing time to rest for breakfast, lunch, the customary afternoon nap, and dinner. Depending on time and place, there were also mid-morning and mid-afternoon refreshment breaks, recognising the value of this rest and nourishment.

We are transitioning from the Third Industrial Revolution of the internet, computers and mobiles, into the fourth Industrial Revolution. Interestingly, it is described as *"the blurring of boundaries between the physical, digital, and biological worlds, a fusion of advances in artificial intelligence (AI), robotics, the Internet of Things (IoT), 3D printing, genetic engineering, quantum computing, and other technologies"*.

We see ourselves constantly exposed to artificial light, the blue light from our mobiles, televisions and computers, affecting our eyesight and interfering with the pineal gland function; a disturbance and incoherence of our circadian rhythm of rest and restore, our autonomic nervous system that naturally repairs our cells.

Our days are prolonged, pushing through our natural rhythms and hormonal cycles of rest, "going against our grain", as we dig deeper and push through. Society calls for action over quietness, causing friction and further de-regulation of our nervous systems, and thus our health and wellbeing. This is further exacerbated by our disconnection to the Earth, a constant membrane underneath our feet, staying in our home and offices, especially when cold and the lure of escapism from computer games and on demand television series.

Somewhere along the lines through our generations, we have falsely come to believe that our worth is materialised by what our output is!

Somehow our existence and value is subject to how busy we are!

That by simply being us, as ourselves is not enough!
That we have to prove our existence and our worthiness!
That rest is a weakness and non-productive and to be guilty of!
That being in our gentle, quieter feminine energy is vulnerable and weak!
That self-care is selfish!

This hard drive and non-grounded way of living came to most people as a crescendo and collapse in 2020. A massive emergency stop button was pressed, where a large number fell off this conveyor belt of society, and questioned its value and purpose to their happiness.

We intuitively flocked to Mother Earth to somehow find inner peace and calm, unbeknown, we were finding the most natural way to ground our nervous system; to receive free electrons to reduce our oxidative stress. We saw the fragility and beauty of our Earth, the health of the planet and ourselves, and our intrinsic relationship.

To take from this, would be how we can flow through life with more ease and grace, how we can be less rigid in our thoughts, patterns and routines. To create pattern breakers as we recognise that every moment is a cycle, from seconds to seasons, a dance between our duality of energies.

To be in our masculine energy, the "doing-driven-focused" energy, to then holding space for stillness, in our feminine, to rest and restore.

This stillness gifts us the clarity of mind, our purpose, connecting to our creative energy and desires, to ensure we are aligned to what serves us joy; to shift then back to our masculine, in a state of trust and allowing these cycles to transition and transmute.

30.

BINDU – THE APEX OF CONNECTION

The interesting relationship of the carotid plexus of the brow chakra, which includes the Arrector Pili muscles that make our hairs stand on end through the connection to the dermal tissue, our skin, which is represented by the crown chakra, sparked further thinking!

I believe this is the bridge from our brow chakra, the pineal gland, to our crown chakra that connects our body as whole, to the universe and our higher self, our soul.

Have you had moments of when you have a thought and get a tingling down from the back of the head and down the spine?

I get these quite regularly, often extends down my limbs as well, as I hold a quietness to experience this wave of sensation through my body. It has an awakening feeling, like my skin and deeper is opening and waking up. These moments I take or perceive as confirmation of my thoughts, it is a yes to what I was thinking and also forming a deep energetic connection to the universal field.

There is an energy centre rather than a chakra located at the back of the head, where the parietal and the occiput cranium bones join, called the Bindu, which translates in Sanskrit as point, or drop and represented by the moon.

This point has much importance in Tantra Yoga, as it is said to be the fountain of eternal youth, the drop "Amrita", nectar of immortality which is activated by the pineal gland physically. I believe this nectar is melatonin, and this life elixir for our body, we would not only prolong our life, but also enjoy perfect health.

However, if the throat chakra Vishuddhi, which is responsible for the purification and detoxification of the body, if not balanced and open, it is unable to capture these drops of nectar. Instead they fall into the fire of the solar plexus and is burned away, causing illness and dis-ease.

This relates to how I understand pain, illness and later dis-ease as heat and inflammation, the breaking down of coherence and communication of the body, unable to heal due to confusion and dispelling of energy, alongside the imbalance of detoxification of toxins and impurities.

In the Gheranda Samhitā (Verses 28-30) it is written:
"The Sun is in the navel and the moon in the head. The nectar that comes from the moon is consumed by the sun, and the life force is gradually used up in this way."

The representation of the moon and the sun in Ayurveda is the masculine and feminine, the Ida and Pingala, the coming together to create the whole.

It may also relate to the hormones melatonin, a powerful anti-inflammatory and antioxidant secreted by the pineal gland, mostly at night - the moon; and serotonin during the day – the Sun. 90% of serotonin is produce in the enteric system, our gut, and is the precursor for melatonin synthesis, and vice versa, both are imperative for homeostasis of the body's key functions.

The Bindu point also overlays the straight sinus that connects the third ventricle deep within the brain, which incorporates the pineal gland, and where it meets at the base of the cranium bones. Connecting to the subarachnoid space (formed between the arachnoid mater and pia mater) containing the cerebrospinal fluid (CSF).

CSF links to the crown chakra as it protects and supports the brain and spinal cord as a cushioning, it is vital for homeostasis of the brain; balancing pH; CO_2 levels; providing nutrients and eliminating toxins. It is the communication carrier of messages, our hormones to our body as a whole, our endocrine system, demonstrating how the pineal gland communicates and influences the pituitary gland which relate to both the brow and crown chakras.

There is also a connection from the subarachnoid space to the bony labyrinth of the inner ear, via the peri-lymphatic duct, where the perilymph is continuous with the cerebrospinal fluid. The image of the third eye by the Egyptians has a spiral at the end; this may well be the representation of the labyrinth of the ear.

31.

CEREBROSPINAL FLUID –
"Our Highly Gifted Juice"

CSF was known by ancient physicians, Hippocrates (460–375 BC) commented on "water" surrounding the brain when describing congenital hydrocephalus, a condition of newborn babies with infections of spina bifida. Galen (130–200AD referred to "excremental liquid" in the ventricles of the brain from where it is purged into the nose.

It was then forgotten for circa sixteen centuries, until Emanuel Swedenborg (1688–1772), a mining engineer fascinated by finding streams deep within the earth, went on a search for the seat of the soul. He referred to CSF as "spiritual lymph" and "highly gifted juice".

The brain is 80-85% water, which enables it to feel like only 25-30 grams, rather than its full mass of 1.4-1.5kg, this is thanks to the Cerebrospinal Fluid. It is a clear and colourless liquid that surrounds and protects the central nervous system (CNS). Consisting of 99% water and 1% is proteins, electrolytes, neurotransmitters, and glucose. Encompassing this, is the Dura Mater, which envelopes the spinal cord from the sacral vertebrae S2 to the foramen magnum, which is the opening in the base of the skull that connects the spinal cord to the brain.

Our sacrum tilts posteriorly when we inhale, and anteriorly when we exhale. Our cranium opens on inhale, propagating a wave of body and pulses, which flows in a rostral direction, (towards the nose/beak front of the head) and then caudally, (to the back of the head and down to the sacrum).

There are currently many theories of how the CSF flows around our bodies, be they respiration, heart rate and its electromagnetic field, convection, diffusion and energy conduction. Maybe they all have an effect, as ultimately CSF will be a connector of all of our systems, so they naturally will have an effect in return.

The key would be coherence as a whole, otherwise confusion and resistance would result, which is why mind-heart coherence is vital for our health, as it acts as a regulator and conductor. This has been studied greatly by the Heart Math Institute.

If I was a betting person, I would go for the hearts electromagnetic torus field, in coherence with the pineal gland and its relationship with the mitochondria in each of the trillion of cells. The energy conducted by the solution of CSF in constant communication and biofeedback with the internal and external energetic world, our Earth's magnetic field.

Within twelve hours, the CSF will have completed the full circuit; it forms part of our very own body clock, also known as the circadian rhythm, which is controlled by our pineal gland. I wonder somehow, whether it has a marker to know it has completed the twelve hour, circuit to then continue the cycle. I would imagine it will have something to do with the hormone released by the pineal gland melatonin and serotonin, our night and day hormones, and the levels of sunlight itself.

Studies have shown that the rhythms of activity in all biological organisms, both plants and animals, which would include us humans too, are closely linked to the gravitational tides created by the orbital mechanics of the sun-Earth-moon system.

The studies showed that the animals modulated their behaviour in tune with the ebb and flow of the tides, in a cycle of approximately 12.4 hours that derived from luna-solar dynamics; a mirroring of the cycle of the cerebrospinal fluid -drawing links to the Bindu point of the Moon nectar and the Sun.

In an adult there is circa 150ml of CSF, and 125ml circulate the system replacing itself every 6-8 hours, producing 400-600ml per day.

The percentage of water in both blood and CSF highlights the relationship with the heart and sacral chakra, as water is the carrier of wisdom, our feminine sacred energy and our emotions. This is where we can link how our emotions are energy-in-motion, the water being the carrier and vital part of the CSF, which is part of our internal communication system, influencing each cell as it comes into contact.

Cerebrospinal fluid is a solution containing key electrolytes, magnesium, calcium, sodium and potassium and the protein albumin that provides energy to the brain. Combined with water, it conducts energy creating an inductive field within and around our body, our very own bio-field; our head being North, and our perineum as South. As a whole we are our very own magnets and depending on our electrical charge, through thoughts and emotional frequencies, determine what we repel and attract, as energy-attracts-energy!

With heart felt awareness and Mindful intentions we become super attractors, within the energetic world of potentiality.

CSF is also an imperative link to our Earth and the element of water and the importance of the quality of the water we drink. Many studies have shown how water holds memory of what it has been in contact with. From its journey and the cycle of evaporation, condensation, precipitation, filtering and collecting. Everything that decomposes and is part of the Earth becomes held within the water, which we drink and is vital for the functions of our mind and body.

The whole wisdom of Earth is held in water, which cycles and flows through our bodies and mind. Somewhere within, we hold memories of all that has been on our Earth, our ancestors, even the dinosaurs! It is even thought that the water that we have on Earth has travelled through the universe to be where it is now. Imagine the potentiality if we connected to this expansive wisdom of Earth and the Universe, what has been here all along in our existence and humanity!

Can it really be that simple; that all we ever need to know is already within us, that it is a matter of trusting this and to tune into ourselves, our sensations, our deep neural and energetic connections?

Yes I believe it is, the aspect of surrendering to this and trusting in oneself, un-peeling all the old beliefs and patterns to access this nectar and inner wisdom, is the journey! Holding the awareness as to what is pure and what is impure, is key. What we allow in and what we choose to release; what serves us purpose and what does not, is the discernment of the mind and heart.

An interesting woman to follow would be Veda Austin – she uses cystography to show the intelligence and the Soul of Water, how through showing images, playing music and words, water will reflect back in a way that blows the mind!

Our ancestors believed that water carries the souls of all that have lived on our Earth, and many sacred sites will be connected to water in some way. The River Avon in the UK, connects Stonehenge, Woodhenge and Durrington Walls!

Are we simply recycling our own bullshit and belief systems?!

The quality of our drinking water, the recycling of our own excrement, what our bodies have chosen to release, including hormones, returns to us through the imprint in water. It is no wonder we continue the patterns and beliefs, as this water feeds the vibration of its own frequency! In addition to this, we have higher levels of hormone due to birth control, fluoride, chloride, plastics, and herbicides.

The high levels of water in the CSF and the brain, highlights the importance of hydration for optimum function of our minds. We also must consider the physical level of the vast number of impurities and chemicals that are within our water. The plastic, the herbicides and pesticides that run off from our soil for food production, the air pollution grounded by the water cycle of rain, and even the chemicals used to "clean" our water. Most likely a contributing factor to why we are seeing an increase in numbers of auto immune diseases, and progressive neurologic disorders such as Alzheimer's disease.

I would be most interested if there was a study to show how drinking pure spring water, with a higher alkaline base, would actually show an improvement in mental wellbeing, clarity and a greater perspective on life. Not just from a hydration perspective, yet also, from the vibration that the water holds in its purity, absorbed into every cell, including the blood and brain.

I drink filtered water as much as possible, and when I remember, I set the intention with the water to bless it, to hold it near to my heart and thank the water for giving me all that I need, and releasing all that I do not. With the work by Dr Masaru Emoto, Veda Austin and others, we are beginning to understand how our intent can change the structure of water.

Now more than ever are our boundaries absolutely fundamental for our health and wellbeing!

Boundaries are represented by the Crown chakra, although the mind and body has many gateways and boundaries acting as the bouncers for each cell, tissue and organs, which relate to the other chakras.

I believe it is our energetic conscious and subconscious thoughts that create and establish these boundaries, in our physical lives and our body. Depending on our discernment of mind, permits the function of these key barriers, our self-worth being part of that!

It sets out the blueprint and foundation of our internal world, within our organs, mind and body, seen as inflammation, pain and dis-ease; and our external world through the energetic connections in our relationships, and those we come in contact with on a daily basis.

Physical inflammation in pain and illnesses, imbalances in relationships, and not attracting the "right" or more so, the "desired" interactions and experiences, highlights our need to address our boundaries, energetically, emotionally, mentally and physical.

To evaluate what old beliefs, patterns and energetic connections we are carrying in our present moment; each time making the choice of what we wish to continue to carry with us, and what we do not, of what serves us joy and purpose and all that does not.

Many of these lay deep in our subconscious mind, from our early years and formation. Stress and trauma experienced in this life and our energetic coding, that imprinted within our genes, through generations right back to whenever we began.

Patterns of abuse through generations are easily seen, many others are subtle and naked to our eyes, yet deeply felt and re-enacted in our triggered thoughts, responses and actions. However, when we become aware in the seat of our perception, allowing ourselves to hold an objectivity of life, we become empowered to break these patterns that are playing out in our lives, drawing a line in the sand through conscious choices.

On another level, when we recognise ourselves as energetic beings that are infinite, and as energy cannot be destroyed, only changed in form. We can start to open up to the possibilities of previous life experiences as a soul, and the energetic attachments made, affecting our present moment; described as Karma in Sanskrit, which translates as an action, work, or deed, and its effect or consequences.

Once again, with awareness and intention to heal, we permit ourselves to heal our karmic wheel on our Earth lineage, our ancestors and our Soul lineage, our previous incarnations.

To do this, we need to consciously dive deep into our energetic coding, our subconscious, and to trust our bodies, our higher self to heal us that is comfortable.

I do this through breath, connecting to my heart, becoming fully grounded into my body, setting an intention and thanking my body, and the universe, for revealing to me what I need to know, and what it needs from me today.

Forming part of one's self care daily practice, which is why they are included in the LOVE2Heal movement meditations as part of the online course.

Zach Bush MD, a physician who specialises in internal medicine and endocrinology, has a beautiful way in explaining how we are nature and energy all as one.

"Every one of us has a continuous energetic center that cannot be destroyed. Every millionth of a second, your energy steps into your physical body as an expression of life... an expression that is You!
But below the visible surface, you are a much deeper beam of light. Any sense of solidity, be it your hand or your face, is the result of a quantum phenomenon - you exist as both a wave and particle at the same time. You are an expression of something much greater than any physical nature ever described or witnessed. So trust that."

32.

THE CROWN AND SACRAL RELATIONSHIP

We cannot gain from others what we do not have, nor give to ourselves!

Waves are energy in motion – Water is the carrier of energy creating waves and flow in our bodies.

I believe it is the magnetic energetic life force working through the medium of water, within the Cerebrospinal Fluid from crown to sacral.

The intensity of a wave - The greater the amplitude of vibration of the particles within the medium, the greater the rate of which the energy is transported through it and the more intense the sound waves.

Our bodies are the medium, our emotions are the amplitude and vibration, the energy is our life force, the sound is our expression and interaction with the universal field. It is our subconscious voice calling our external experiences. Our joy, love and peace is an internal journey first!

We cannot receive external experiences unless our internal world resonates at that frequency and amplitude first. We cannot gain from others, which we do not have or give to ourselves.

Upon this insight we are able to shift our perspective, we navigate ourselves away from the victim to the empowered.

If you seek more compassion and respect from others, in your relationships, then dive deeper, and hold that compassion and respect for yourself. Express you healthy boundaries from your sacral, heart and throat chakras, which create and uphold this compassionate space for you.

Go within and see what wounds are reappearing for your healing. Is it space for you inner child, do they need to be heard, do they need to feel safe and supported, do they need more love and acceptance of self?

Life is energy and mirrors reflecting back to us, to see our truth within our pure essence. We are constantly interacting and exchanging with one another and holding mirrors up for us to see.

To see all aspects of ourselves, our inner being; our soul; our purpose; our gifts; our love; our wounds; our pain; our fears; our ego; our beauty; our magnificence and our light.

To come to a space of acceptance and love for ourselves as one; a wholeness, an inner peace and contentment, the jigsaw and puzzle of life coming together with ease, enabling us to see from a rounded and open perspective.

The gift we can give ourselves and others is space, a safe supportive space from our hearts, for one another to explore and self-reflect with no judgement; awareness and observation of self, guiding us to make heart conscious choices on what we wish to see, feel and be in this world.

Imagine the conversations we could have, if we all walked and talked with a higher state of consciousness, appreciating that the wounds and beliefs are simply being reflected back to us to heal. Soon enough I am sure we wouldn't feel these wounds, and we would evolve as humanity, with greater humility.

When waves meet the bottom of the sea bed, a boundary, friction causes it to slow down.

As we open, heal and balance our chakras through listening and observing our bodies, our emotions, our fears and our patterns; coherence is formed through our spine, our central nervous system. Stabilising our life force to reach every cell, to give and receive in balance. To enable pure health of each of the trillion of cells that vibrates in our body.

To receive the life force of energy and nutrients, to restore our individual health, taking what it needs and then allowing it to pass though on to the neighbouring cells.

To have the physical discernment to release impurities, our own by-products, and the environmental toxins into the interstitial fluid, also known as tissue fluid, the liquid that surrounds our cells.

The fluid filters out of our blood vessels and into our body's cells, to deliver essential nutrients, while simultaneously removing waste products- our lymphatic system.

Sound is the vibration of energy being the platform of coherence. The sound waves carry the messages of order and balance throughout the body instantaneously; they awaken cells that have been closed to release what no longer serves them, this movement and expansion awakens the light that is within each cell.

Awakening our waves of energy, allows us to release our stagnancy in mind and body, stimulating the lymphatic system that requires the expansion and contraction to create the wave and force to flow.

When each chakra balance and support one another, it creates harmony and coherence. We are able to release our un-serving fears, thoughts, emotions and beliefs, to enable us to feel strong in ourselves, fully embodied and acceptance of who we are.

A vessel of light and love, and to have the courage to be the full expression of such, growing brighter, with the understanding that moments of contraction and going inward is a gateway towards greater expansion and expression.

33.

WHAT IS YOUR TRUTH?

*If our truth is based upon our perception
and our perspective can change…
Then what is our truth?*

Even though everything in the universe appears to look different, it all comes from the same energy—it just vibrates at a different speed so it exists on a different frequency, which either makes it tangible or intangible.

It is beyond our perceptions of time, of infinite possibilities without restrictions or limitations, the frequency of infinite abundance, represented by the element of light as it connects to the unified energy field, which we are a part of.

We as in our human forms, are a denser collection of these atoms, quarks, neurons, protons and photons, creating what we perceive as matter. We are a duality of the electromagnetic fields that combine into a single physical field, which is beautifully depicted by the lotus flower, with two petals joining together by a triangle or prism.

I certainly do not profess to be a quantum physicist, however, when we start to open our mind, to understand how our wonderful miraculous bodies and minds are formed. A creation of collective energetic intelligence, gathering in absolute precision to create us, and the same source of energies are orchestrated to create all creatures of the Earth.

We start to open our minds to be aware of our old un-serving perceptions and beliefs, that we are separate from each other, living on a planet rather than being part of the planet.

We start to see that we all are individually a symphony of these energies, yet in a denser form. A collective of "tighter knitted" vibrational energies, our bodies, a collaboration of miraculous individuals, a spectrum of light from the same source of life, which for us to understand and to try to comprehend, are described in language as God, the Devine, the Creator, the Source.

However, unfortunately the need for descriptive labels as part of our language has caused separation. Due to the attachment to our belief of self and ancestral beliefs, that continues through the lineage of generations. Our primitive needs to be accepted and to belong in a tribe; a conditioned thought process that there can only by one right and wrong, which feeds judgement and division. Dividing society with conflicting and different beliefs, becoming a need to prove oneself and to convince others "to see the light" of their beliefs!

This systematically, has been in our society for generations and thousands of years, represented through religion, politics, race geographically and colour, sex, age and even down to what sports team one follows.

Just sit with this for a moment. It certainly "blows the mind", for me it felt and still does, like my head expanded, a sensation that a part of me opened and lifted from my mind, an illumination; an opportunity to see and perceive things differently, yet totally throwing me off my "known" centre.

This may be an uncomfortable experience, to feel an unraveling of what felt like our truths, our known self, are actually not! Initiating a process of an unlearning of the learning, and a relearning process all at once, a shedding of skin inside out, creating the opportunity to regrow, thus forms an objective awareness of self, our perceptions and actions.

I have conducted part of my life with a perception that we are all separate bodies going about our business and worlds within the world. Our life is ours to control, and what happens to someone else the other side of the world doesn't affect us. That we are physical matter using our energy trying to get from A to B, with the space of time between, and that all is separate to us to attain.

The need for language, of labels, beliefs, and patterns to bring communication, a sense of order and understanding in our minds, is actually what heightens this separation, especially when we attach judgement.

We are all vortices of spinning energy in layers of frequency, which are described as our chakras. The base chakra being the lower denser frequency grounding us to Mother Earth, through the Earth Star, becoming a wider higher frequency as it ascends through the chakras to the Crown, yet remaining interwoven with a representation of each within, which we see as a rainbow, from red to blue-purple.

Imagine oneself and others feeding from this unified field, creating our own energy vortices, shaped like a whirlwind with the cone pointing and connecting to Earth, opening as it reaches the sky and sun.

Picture your base of the cone being magnetised by the core of the Earth, grounding and centring; exchanging energy between the two, giving the stability, framework and boundaries for the energy fields within, to be in coherence; expressing their frequency within balance of one another, similar to a graceful spinning top.

These healthy boundaries create the space for the frequencies, our chakra and energy centres, to expand and express, to reach up and ascend to the sky; opening and receiving the light from our sun and the universe, filtering through each layer in open communication, flow and ease.

Then add people, other vortices also in balance and coherence, with awareness of each other, each knowing the effect we have on this unified field of energy, that is our connection to our life force; acknowledging and respecting each other's boundaries, with the intention to support one another in kindness and compassion,

How does this image feel to you, does it create peace, calm a feeling of mutual respect and compassion for others, a feeling that there are no limits when we connect to this unified infinite energy field?

Recognising that the limits we place upon ourselves are only our conditioned perceptions and beliefs, thus the abundance of opportunities are simply waiting for us to imagine and create, "the sky has no limits".

Now imagine you as a spinning top without the base of grounding and centring, what does it do? Well, it either does not spin and loses its energy, or it goes off in a chaotic non-coherent way, bouncing all over the place, similar to a pinball machine, with no real compass vision or control of direction.

Now add in other people as these vortices of electromagnetic energies, some greater in energy and force, some fuelled by fear with the intention to control others and to absorbed others energy and light, and those in subconscious chaos.

Whilst we are grounded and centred, we can see this chaos for what it is, and have the choice as to whether to be part of it. Either becoming overwhelmed in a dis-coherent state of mind and body, or we remain within our healthy boundaries. Navigating through the storms that others generate, not feeding our energy to such and creating the energy and pathways we wish to see and be, with an ease and grace to our steps in the dance of life.

Yet imagine what happens without your grounding and rooting, you become off balance and pulled/magnetised into these greater forces. With no boundaries, absorbing energy that is not yours into the layers of the physical, emotional and mental, and losing your energy and power to others. Becoming bewildered and overwhelmed, swept away with such, lacking a compass and direction in one's life, possibly feeling out of control with no purpose or joy, that life is just too hard.

Which one are you?

Oxidative Stress, Finding Our Balance and Boundaries

How this translates into our lives, health and wellbeing, is whether we are living in a calm, graceful coherent state, or of stress and dis-coherence. Naturally, life will flow and interlace between both states of being, yet it is within our power to breathe and create a space of coherence, to allow our bodies to heal, and eliminate what no longer serves us.

Allowing our bodies to find homeostasis and balance, with each cell communicating to every other cell, to nourish, repair and release, via the mitochondria and biophotons of light within.

Take this to our cellular level; for us to wake up in the morning, our bodies need to transition from the healing parasympathetic nervous system of sleep, to the sympathetic nervous system that fires our bodies into awareness, to operate our body and metabolism.

The by-products of this normal essential metabolic process, are free radicals or reactive oxygen species (ROS). Produced by each of our trillion cells and controlled by the mitochondria. This is compounded by exposure to external sources, such as X-rays, ozone, cigarette smoking, vaping, air pollutants, and industrial chemicals.

Cells are composed of molecules, which in turn are composed of one or more atoms joined by chemical bond. Each atom to be stable, needs to be paired in balance of protons (positive), electrons (negative) and neurons (neutral), and if the outer layer of the atom called the shell is not, it will connect to other atoms to complete its outer shell. Stealing electrons and protons and destabilising the other atom, becoming an unstable free radical that reacts with other atoms.

Normally, the bonds between each healthy atom within the boundary of the shell, can be split during metabolism, leaving two equal atoms in balance of paired electrons and protons. Imbalance occurs, when free radicals bond with lipids, proteins, and other molecules in the body.

When oxygen molecules split into single atoms that have unpaired electrons, they become unstable free radicals that seek other atoms, or molecules to bind. If this continues to happen, it begins a process called oxidative stress, Reactive Oxygen Species. (ROS).

In normal circumstances, the body provides endogenous substances (within the cell) free-radical scavengers, or anti-oxidants to combine with the free radicals.

Should there be a reduction of these scavengers/anti-oxidants and/ or, an overproduction of free radicals from stress and toxins, the radicals donate to, or steal an electron from another molecule. This leads to a chain reaction that triggers more free radicals.

The chain reaction results in damage to the cell membrane and deoxyribonucleic acid (DNA), altered enzyme reactions, and damage to collagen and connective tissues.

Various studies and theories have connected oxidative stress and to free radicals, to:

Central nervous system diseases, such as Alzheimer's and other dementias, Diabetes; Cardiovascular disease due to clogged arteries; Autoimmune and inflammatory disorders; Rheumatoid arthritis and cancer; Cataracts and age-related vision decline; Age-related changes in appearance, such as loss of skin elasticity, wrinkles, greying hair, hair loss, and changes in hair texture; Genetic degenerative diseases, such as Huntington's disease or Parkinson's.

Nutrition is most important, as Vitamins C, and E, glutathione, beta-carotene, and plant oestrogen called phytoestrogens, are among the many antioxidants that may cancel out the effects of free radicals.

Exercise and the right food choices are required for optimum function of the methylation cycle, of metabolism and detoxing. These nutrients are vital, choline, betaine, methionine, folate, vitamins B12 and B6, as well as certain minerals like magnesium, zinc and sulfur. These can be found in leafy greens, cruciferous vegetables, beet, seeds, rosemary, berries, turmeric, tea, liver, beans and legumes.

34.

WHAT IS YOUR FREQUENCY?

"What's the frequency, Kenneth?" is your Benzedrine, uh-huh
I was brain-dead, locked out, numb, not up to speed
I thought I'd pegged you an idiot's dream
Tunnel vision from the outsider's screen

Lyrics by R.E.M

The labyrinth is the innermost part of the ear, it contains two important parts; the cochlea, which connects the middle and outer ear, relaying sounds to the brain and is responsible for hearing.

The second is the vestibular system, also known as the inner ear, which is a complex set of fluid-filled channels and otolith organs, which contain small crystals of calcium carbonate (calcite), found in the pineal gland and our bones.

They respond to gravitational forces, also called gravity receptors, which contribute to our sense of balance and our spatial relationship with the world. If compressed, or displaced, possibly through cranial tension and trauma, we may experience dizziness, tinnitus, vertigo, disequilibrium, unsteadiness, nausea, disorientation, and occasionally a "spacey" or detached feeling.

It is thought however, intermittent high pitched ringing in the ears without the pain and discomfort, are higher energetic fields oscillating with our energy fields, to communicate and open connections to our higher self, our third eye- our pineal gland -our command centre.

If you are experiencing such, it may be worth taking moments of stillness, such as meditation or being in nature. Listen quietly, to be open to wisdom beyond one's own thoughts. I like to say *"thank you Universe, for revealing to me what I need to know today"* and then listen with objectivity and non-attachment and with no conscious expectation. Similar to when we forget something and we are racking our brains to remember, it is only in the forgetting and releasing the need to remember, that we remember!

The term "spatial relationships" refers to the way objects are arranged in relation to one another in geographic space. This can be reflected not just physically, yet also emotionally, energetically and spiritually, in how we see our place and position in this world, which relates to the Crown chakra, becoming active between 20-27 years, as we fully react and interact with the world.

This cycle as the chakra is opened, becoming active and dominant in our lives, raises questions such as *"Why am I here? What is my purpose in life? What is the purpose of life, there must be more to life than this?!"*

This opening and stirring of this energetic field, ultimately leads us to explore our inner fulfillment and contentment, to seek our Soul purpose. For when we are living, actioning and flowing in alignment to our heart based Soul purpose, we are naturally in joy, and in connection to all that is; beholding a sense of wholeness and inner peace. This is most likely a time of radical change in our life and work, the moment of one's awakening, like a butterfly emerging from its cocoon.

However, it can also lay dormant, ignored and unheard, the inner voice seeking change, to awaken from a spiritual slumber. This may be felt as depression, an unsatisfied emptiness of unfulfilled joy, no matter of one's attempt to fill from external stimuli, of materialism and experiences.

The inner voice of change will often be quietened by our ego, our old un-serving restrictive patterns and beliefs, which leaves us frozen in fear of the unknown; to not look or venture within, a fear to see, hear and feel our inner pain and emptiness.

It is the moment of light, the opening of our brow chakra around our adolescent years, when we come to understand that these thought patterns and emotions are not actually our truth, they are just illusions keeping us "safe" in our confinement.

Imagine a butterfly never releasing itself from the cocoon, how so much beauty and potential to be shared within this world, lost to fear and a lack of curiosity and courage.

"A butterfly is a flowering of a caterpillar beyond its wildest dreams, held within the power of trust in self"

This is the beginning of the inner journey of understanding, awareness and discernment of what is pure and serving. A surrendering and unburdening of what you no longer need to carry. With love, acceptance and a sense of worthiness, to open to what your desire to experience, to feel, see and be in this world; receiving the nourishment, physically, emotionally and spiritually.

This inner journey leads to a deep grounded space of trust in self and all that is, held consciously within the axis of a coherent heart and mind. An inner stabilising platform upon which we flow, expand and evolve, interacting and interlacing with our outer world.

Similar to the musical scales where each octave returns to the start note. From the Crown, we return to the Base chakra, establishing a deeper sense of inner support and safety, rather than seeking externally, with this deeper and more profound conscious awareness.

Enabling us to make aligned choices with our desires, joy and pleasure of the sacral chakra, our creativity; our Solar Plexus – the aligned actions towards our goals; our heart and upwards, as an expression of. The cycle repeats like a symphony, to realign and reconfigure, unfolding opportunities within awareness to renew, heal, repair, and a state of wholeness and embodiment, as we honour each aspect of ourselves.

35.

HEALING IS SKIN DEEP

The crown chakra relates to our skin. Via the cutaneous sensory fibres within the skin, it conveys changes in temperature, pH, and inflammatory mediators to the cerebrum of the central nervous system.

As life forms as an embryo, from the first primitive cells, the ectoderm, mesoderm and endoderm, (which link to particular areas of our body), the next miracle around *day 15,* sees a visible centralisation and coherence of the cells, the beginning of the central nervous system, called the primitive streak.

As the cells multiply and form tubes, these loop and link back within themselves, the inner tube becoming the neural tube of the central nervous system and the outer layer of our skin. When we are born, it is the change of environment as we pass through the compression of the vaginal passage, which prepares the baby to crown and expand into the big wide world.

Felt through the skin, the autonomic nervous system is activated to take our first instinctive breath, and to seek safety through the connection and unification with our Mother – demonstrating the infinite loop of the chakras, from crowning, to *rooting* to the breast!

This intrinsic relationship highlights the inherent need of humans for touch and connection, which is vital for regulation of our nervous systems and heart rate variability. Our birth and the moments after, become deeply imprinted and form the foundations of our relationship and connection to the outer world.

Any traumas experienced by Mother and baby in birth, including C-sections; tensions within the cranium from being stuck; use of forceps; the cord around our neck; and compression of the most *"simpler"* births, affect and influence our body as a whole.

If untreated, these tensions and trauma will influence us in how we are now, our ability to cope with stress, our musculoskeletal system, our digestion, our ability to connect with others, how we breathe and if we like to be touched.

This is why cranial work is so important and effective for all newborns- personally I feel this should be available to all, within weeks of being born, to avoid many issues in later life, let alone "colic" and sleep for the infants.

The evolving circuit of the skin-fascia-neural connection is like a body sock, a mould upon which we grow within and re-generate from. Highlighting, the importance of regular self-care and treatments mind and body, especially through the connective tissue, the fascia, as it releases these tensions, returning to its natural health and structure.

The skin is the principle visual organ of boundaries, the physical encapsulation of our internal world, and the relationship and interaction of the external world. Any issues of our skin relates to our relationship and boundaries of both, be they physically, emotionally and energetically.

The skin holds the integral wisdom and discernment as to what is pure and impure, it absorbs and releases, most similar to the small intestine, the gut/brain barrier, it is another vital barrier for our health. Issues of the gut, such as imbalanced gut flora and microbiome, will be represented by the health of our skin, such as eczema. Likewise, chemicals in skin care and perfumes can affect our gut biome.

Thoughts to consider-

Are your boundaries weakened by patterns of lack of self-worth, allowing external influences, environment and people to irritate and inflame you, *to get under one's skin!?*

Are you too closed to receive, preventing nourishment from the external to the internal, causing dryness, shrinking away and detachment? Have you become reserved and detached from life, maybe carrying hurt and grief?

Are your boundaries closed, blocking to receive due to hurt, however, unable to forgive and let go? A fire that pushes away, restricting the skin to release what no longer serves, found in abscesses or an overflow of toxins, anger and inflammation, such as acne?

The locations of symptoms are relative due to the somatic and dermal tissues relationship.

For instance the face; what do you need to face up to?

The feet and lower limbs are where you are going in life, are you in alignment? Are you being pushed down a path you do not wish to be on? Also relating to support, holding our place and presence in the world, do we feel safe, is there a sense of exposure?

Our arms and hands are what we are holding onto, they are closely connected to our heart by the fascia, thus any symptoms would relate to our ability to receive and to let go. Trust and forgiveness will certainly play a role here.

Interestingly, these are the furthest points away from the heart – maybe these are points in the body, that the heart is keeping at its distance, to push away to preserve itself in fear, yet also stopping to receive!

The groin and the skin of our pleasure organs relate to our intimate relationship with self.

Understanding the somatic relationship, of skin and the nervous system, is a map for us to see where the inflammation and tensions are, of mind and heart.

Where do we Begin and where do we End?
Are we Finite Moments within Infinity?

The Crown is the unification, the oneness, the interaction with our physical self to our higher/spiritual self, and the unified field of consciousness, and how we interact within both.

Our internal frequency influencing and creating our external experiences, and vice versa, to the point when both merge as one, through the energetic boundaries of thought, past, present and future.

Beyond our physical body, we also have seven energetic field bodies that form our Aura, which interlace with each seven chakras. They act as an energetic boundaries and protective shells around the body, likened to the ozone layer around the Earth.

The Earth's visible Aura or corona (Latin for crown) is a rainbow, greater still in the Aurora Borealis and Aurora Australis (the Northern and Southern lights).

What I find most intriguing is the cycles of seven, the seven chakras and the crown being the seventh chakra, the seven layers of the skin, which relates to the crown and the seven energetic bodies.

When you take the seven chakras, and times by the seven skin layers, by the seven energetic bodies it equals – 7x7x7 = 343

In numerology you seek the one digit whole number by adding, so 3+4+3 = 10; 1+0 = 1.

Hence, these seven aspects layering upon one another come back to the number 1, the oneness, wholeness, coming back to where it started.

For me, this is about unpeeling the layers, physically, emotionally, mentally, spiritually and energetically; past, present and future. Energy is not linear as we perceive it by our conditions of time. We are cycles of infinite energy, changing in form and density to points of singularity from the same source.

I have found that our miraculous bodies are actually portals of time for us to consciously connect with, past, present or future; to alchemise through intention and emotional consciousness.

Therefore to heal, and to come to a state of wholeness in our present, we must recognise all aspects of ourselves, as energetic being, including our Earth and Soul lineage.

Skin of radiance – Beauty is Skin Deep

Our skin is our first physical boundary and holds the energetic layers of our aura, the energy bodies, and the chakras. Therefore, our skin is a great indicator of our health. Have we become too weathered by our outside environment, have we placed too much importance on our relationship to the outside world?

Studies have found that certain photoreceptor cells located in the retina, can detect light even in people who do not have the ability to see.

The results confirm that the brain can detect light in the absence of working vision. They also suggest that light can quickly alter brain activity through pathways unrelated to sight.

"*The researchers suggest that this nonvisual light sensing, may aid in regulating many aspects of human brain function, including sleep/wake cycles and threat detection*"- Scientific American.

Skin has a photosensitive system, similar to the one found in the eye. Photosensitive molecules in the skin include biomolecules, endogenous chromophores, pigments and light-sensing proteins called opsins.

Thus, our skin also receives light similar to our eyes, the opsins act as the *"eyes of the skin",* our largest sensory organ!

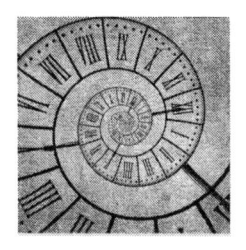

36.

THE PINEAL GLAND

This piece of writing about the pineal gland was actually the last part of the LOVE2Heal chakra content; a feeling of saving the best to last! Alongside the feeling that it holds so much importance I wanted to do it justice. Which also scared me a little, my subconscious, at times of Am I Enough? - *a pattern that is becoming quite boring now! — which is great progress, as I am starting to detach myself from the cycle, and creating a new pattern that is serving me joy and purpose.*

There are two parts to the pineal gland; its internal relationship with our health mind and body, our power to heal; and the external world of others and the universe, our power to manifest.

There is so much mystery and magic about the pineal gland, as research is still uncovering its role and purpose. I believe it is the root and seed of our magick, and once we truly understand its potential, humanity will evolve. Like an opening spiral, connecting purposefully into the cosmos, with the universal field held by our hearts magnetic energy. We begin to create changes to the highest good for us individually and collectively.

We begin to awaken as a collective, to seek love, joy and peace, breaking free from fear that separates and controls us, which has suppressed humanity for thousands of years. To a place of understanding that we are one, our thoughts and actions are like a cosmic wave within the ocean that holds us all.

However, all changes start from within; our external world is the reflection of our internal world, so let us explore this magick bean planted in the centre of our mind.

The pineal gland is a neuroendocrine organ no bigger than a pea, and is the control centre for the endocrine system. Located between the thalamic bodies of the 3rd ventricle, and is bathed in cerebrospinal fluid.

It is part of the diencephalon, that relays sensory information between brain regions, and controls many autonomic functions of the peripheral nervous system. It connects structures of the endocrine system with the nervous system, and works with the limbic system to generate and manage emotions and memories.

It is named due to its shape, like a pinecone, as the pineal gland consists of rods and cones, which is the evolutionary precursor to the flower, their spines spiral, crossing in perfect Fibonacci sequence in either direction, 8 in one direction and 13 in the other.

The Fibonacci sequence and the golden ratio, relate to sacred geometry found in many aspects of nature, such as roses, sunflowers, snails and ammonites. Our body follows the golden ratio from the dimensions of the cranium, our facial structure, to the number of bones in our hands.

Colour wave lengths of the visible light spectrum correspond with the chakras, and colours associated with each other, and the pattern of spaces in between each one is on the golden ratio!

Throughout the ages, a spiral has represented infinite expansion, symbolising the expansion of nature and the universe, reflecting the magical inter-connection of our micro- and macro- cosmos. For centuries, this knowledge was considered sacred, a way of understanding the deeper beauty and spirituality in life.

Interestingly, and unlikely to be just a coincidence, sunflower seeds are rich in tryptophan, an amino acid that is fundamental for the synthesis of melatonin and serotonin within the pineal gland, it is essential fuel for the health of the endocrine gland, thus our whole endocrine system!

Role of the Pineal Gland –

Melatonin – Serotonin and Mitochondria

The Anja chakra means to perceive, "command" or "beyond wisdom" in Sanskrit. My theory is that our bodies have grown from this seed of the pineal gland, our control centre. For the hormones that are produced by the pineal gland, melatonin and serotonin have a fundamental relationship with the mitochondria, our life force within every cell of our body.

The pineal gland communicates through the neurotransmitters, melatonin and serotonin, to the mitochondria within the trillion of cells, to activate and repair.

Alongside the water that becomes the cerebrospinal fluid, the intelligence and held wisdom, the cells cohere with one another to create life itself. Vibrating and synchronising from our primitive cells and as one, follows the blueprint, the seed of life to grow the miracles that we are.

The pineal gland is the conductor ensuring the flow, ease, and connection of the orchestra's symphony, each cell replicating and transforming, to know when each stage has been completed; for instance, as an embryo, the wisdom to know when both arms have created and when to stop.

Writing this, I feel so inspired and in wonder for the miracles that we, for our presence, is a miracle in itself!

So why on Earth do we give ourselves such a hard time, it really is not our truth!

Be present right now and acknowledge the Miracle that You Are.

Key Facts

The pineal gland's sympathetic neural supply, is from the Superior Cervical Ganglion (SCG), which is located at the top of the neck and base of the skull, C1-C4 vertebrae, and posterior to the carotid artery.

The communication branches of the SCG are mainly connected to the Vagus (CN X) and glossopharyngeal nerves (CN IX). These two cranial nerves out of the four, have sensory, motor, and parasympathetic functions, the other two are cranial nerves, the trigeminal nerve and CNVII, the facial nerve.

It would be fair to assume that any impingement of the SCG from neck injuries, whiplash and poor posture from working at a computer, to phone use, could affect the regulation and activation of the pineal gland.

The parasympathetic neural supply to the pineal gland is from the optic ganglia. Our eyes are connected to the pineal gland, from the retina optics, the Optic Chiasm, the part of the brain where the optic nerves cross, where two become one.

Directly above this, is the suprachiasmatic nucleus (SCN), a tiny anterior part of the hypothalamus region of the brain. It is the central pacemaker of the circadian timing system, and regulates most circadian rhythms (daily to seasonal and most likely life cycles) in the body, through photosensitive ganglion cells, stimulating the pineal gland.

Through light and stimulation of the SCN and parasympathetic nerves of the eyes, the healing restorative functions of the pineal gland are stimulated. Regulated by darkness and the decrease of light, the light being received triggers the production of melatonin at night, and serotonin during the day.

Melatonin

Melatonin and serotonin are neurotransmitters and hormones as they both stimulate the brain cells, the nervous system and individual cells. Melatonin is a ubiquitous natural neurotransmitter, which means it is found everywhere within the body, including the cerebrospinal fluid, even behind our eyes, which is stimulated in REM (rapid eye movement)

We experience REM when our brains are in delta wave pattern, during sleep, and in higher states of meditation, connecting to our higher consciousness. I call it a downloading or upgrading, as our brains internally process, playing an important role in dreaming, memory, emotional processing, and healthy brain development.

Melatonin is mostly produced in the early hours 2-3:00am; this is when the pineal gland is considerably active, which may be a factor for disturbed sleep patterns, especially if awakening with creative thoughts and visions. However, a dysfunctional pineal gland could also be at play here, as an enlarged calcified gland will affect the thalamus in autonomic functions, such as temperature control, night sweats being a key symptom, as well as weight gain and mood swings.

Melatonin also regulates the immune system and energy metabolism. It binds to the albumin in our blood, reacting with G-protein receptors, located within the cell membranes, to implement biological intracellular functions needed. It increases the production of ATP (our energy) in control mitochondria, the power house and life force of our cells.

It inhibits oxidative stress, acting as an antioxidant as a free radical scavenger and anti-inflammatory, as it counteracts the cyanide-induced inhibition of ATP. Studies have shown, that melatonin is fundamental in the anti-aging process, and neuroprotective properties, promoting mitophagy (cell repair detoxing) and improves the homeostasis of mitochondria.

Melatonin is our natural anti-oxidant and anti-inflammatory – for our health and wellbeing, it is our individual and collective mission to ensure the health of the pineal gland as one of our top priorities!

I believe melatonin alongside the CSF, is the nectar and elixir that ancient healing has described in the Bindu point.

Serotonin

However, for the mighty melatonin to be synthesised, it needs its counterpart serotonin, aka 5HT. Serotonin is an inhibitory monoamine neurotransmitter that also acts as a hormone. It is vital for the functions of the whole body and our organs; it regulates our mood, sexuality and libido, appetite and pain.

It modulates vasoconstriction/dilation of the cells within the cardiovascular and respiratory (pulmonary) systems; psychomotor functions, which involve the combination of precise motor responses, attention, and cognitive problem-solving abilities.

It regulates our digestion and gastrointestinal control; sleep mechanisms through synthesis of melatonin; regulation of our body temperature, pain and the perception of pain via the hypothalamus; and regulates the parasympathetic neural input to the bladder, which contracts the bladder to urinate.

Serotonin supports energy balance and modulation of the

Hypothalamic Pituitary Adrenal Axis (HPA Axis), regulating our levels of cortisol and adrenaline, that enables us to get up in the morning and function, yet also to reduce stress and inflammation. The raphe nuclei and pineal gland, are the primary locations in the brain for the production of the neurotransmitter serotonin, and the serotonin synthesised in the raphe nuclei is then sent throughout the entire central nervous system.

Once in the gastrointestinal tract, serotonin then takes on hormone and endocrine functions, where it is said that 95% of serotonin is produced by the microbiome of our gut. Highlighting that our gut health is imperative for our overall health! Altered serotonin signalling in the bowel forms disorders such as IBS and IBD.

Seeing Eye to Eye

Both melatonin and serotonin stimulate as neurotransmitters, the secretion of vasopressin and oxytocin from the posterior lobe of the pituitary gland, and is involved in the mediation of the vasopressin and oxytocin response to stress.

Vasopressin, an antidiuretic hormone (ADH), plays essential roles in the control of the body's osmotic balance, blood pressure regulation, sodium homeostasis, and kidney functioning.

Oxytocin, aka the "love hormone", triggers feelings of love and protection, which naturally occurs when parents and children look into one another's eyes, or when they embrace. It enhances relationship bonding through empathy and trust. Oxytocin can induce anti-stress-like effects, such as reduction of blood pressure and cortisol levels. It increases pain thresholds, exerts an anxiolytic-like effect and stimulates various types of positive social interaction.

"Maintaining eye contact creates a calming, connected state of being that, after 30 to 60 seconds, triggers oxytocin," says Linda Jackson, a graduate of WBI's Certificate in Positive Psychology and a presenter at the Embodied Positive Psychology Summit.

There are strong links between the serotonin and dopamine systems, structurally and in function, both are released with eye contact. In some cases, however, serotonin may inhibit dopamine production, which means that low levels of serotonin can lead to an overproduction of dopamine.

Over production of dopamine or too much dopamine concentrated in some parts of the brain, and not enough in other parts, is linked to being more competitive, aggressive and having poor impulse control. It can lead to conditions that include ADHD, binge eating, addiction and gambling.

Interestingly, research shows that phone users scrolling from one post to another on social media every 19 seconds, the brain gets a hit of dopamine each time, creating a sort of neurological 'high', a foundation to addictive behaviour.

If our serotonin levels are reducing due to stress, lack of exercise, poor sleep and diet, are our lifestyles changing to create a quick fix, to increase our 'happiness highs'? For instance, with alcohol, drugs, phones and games, all addictive substitutes to our natural ability to be happy! Coupled with how the blue light from these devices negatively affects the pineal gland, the melatonin and the mitochondria. As well as alcohol sterilising the gut micro biome, and pesticides blocking production of amino acids, which are fundamental for serotonin synthesis.

It becomes a downward spiral of lowering serotonin, increasing dopamine through behaviours that continue the reduction of the serotonin. However, all patterns can be broken through awareness and conscious changes!

Tryptophan

For the mighty serotonin neurotransmitter and hormone to be produced, its precursor is an essential amino acid, tryptophan, a key building block to our endocrine and nervous systems. Tryptophan is not stored in the body; therefore it has to come from our diet; such as cheese, chicken, egg whites, fish, milk, sunflower seeds, peanuts and pumpkin seeds.

It is imperative to have tryptophan in our diet for our health and wellbeing mind and body. It is fundamental for the key neurotransmitters, serotonin and melatonin to exist, to allow our bodies to be able to function on a day to day life, and to bring homeostasis and healing.

Crystal Clear

The pineal gland is made of pinealocytes, which have two types; Type 1, contains serotonin, and type 2 contains melatonin. It is believed that they have evolved from photoreceptor cells, which have a huge biological importance, as they convert light (visible electromagnetic radiation) into signals that can stimulate biological processes.

The photoreceptor proteins in the cell absorb photons, triggering a change in the cell's membrane potential, supporting the natural ability of our cells to repair and rebuild themselves, called photon-light repair. On a physical, emotional and spiritual level, this interestingly could also mean how the cell expresses itself, through its epigenome, realising its full potential and expression.

The health of each cell depends on the ability to receive this pure white light!

Opening the light that is related to our crown chakra, and receiving by our pineal gland, our third eye, holds the space of potential and transformation. We are able to create our physical reality, from our energetics, to our body cells; through our ability to receive light, depending on our perception, of either a "positive or negative light" the angle upon which we view it.

This is a beautiful confirmation of *"A Miracle is a shift of Perception"*, to *"see the light"*, to hold clarity and truth on matters. To see things for what they are, to awaken, to understand the world from a higher perspective, and your role and purpose within. To be grounded and held in the higher energetic space of our hearts, filled with love and acceptance, free from fear.

Picture a prism and light passing through it, the dispersion and full expression of the spectrum of colour held within the white light, is dependent on the angle of refraction. The third eye symbol represented with a downward triangle, three sides to receive from above, our crown and the two sides (the two hemispheres of our brain), to come to the one apex as it disperses inwards, into our body.

Studies have shown that a cell damaged up to 99.9%, can actually repair under a certain frequency of light, called photon light repair. Cacogenic compounds actually refract and block this integral healing light beam that is within us, our natural ability to heal.

Photodynamic therapy (PDT) and other light-based therapies are being used for treating prostate cancer.

"where our attention goes our energy flows!"

How we direct our attention, focus and energy is vital. Imagine our thoughts as energetic light beams pulsing through our mind, refracting and dispersing. Now bring dis-coherence to these bands of light, from the conflicted beliefs systems, emotions, fears and trauma held within the subconscious mind; where 98% of our actions and thoughts derive from on a daily basis. They are our emotional cacogenics- the cancer of our mind!

Imagine the chaos and confusion, the lost energy from overthinking and worrying, as we project our thoughts and attention on aspects outside of our control. The replaying of emotions and past events, like an old vinyl record going round and round, never leaving its track of thought, blocking light to pass through or shift its angle.

If we do not have healthy boundaries of our mind, we are vulnerable to exposure, from the light and chemical pollution of our environment, other people's emotions and their expectations projected upon us, and/or absorbed through patterning.

The light travelling from all angles, refracting and dispersing, loses clarity, clouding our thoughts and judgement. Creating overwhelm of stimuli, a dis-coherence, through the over burning of our solar plexus with fear, regularly stimulated by the subconscious mind and the amygdala. The multi refractions of light become similar to a disco ball, all over the place with no real focus or clarity – aka brain fog, ADHD.

Now imagine a coherence of mind and heart, the heart fully open, centering, balancing and supporting the mind. It brings focus and clarity, our consciousness comes forward, a solid beam of light flows through the axis of our heart and central nervous system grounding at our feet, a coherence of all cells, fundamental to life and repair.

Try it now with your hands on your heart (right over left, the soles of your feet on the ground, and breathe for a few moments, think of what brings you joy and open your heart as if it is your lungs, how does this feel?

This pause upon conscious breathing, allows for self-reflection, and our metaconsciousness to review our thoughts and actions, and how we wish to feel and be in this world, our life and journey. It holds a space, where we can let go of what no longer serves us joy, and breathe in to receive what does, to allow our body to resonate with higher frequency emotions, our energy- in-motion.

Remember the clear light,
The pure clear white light.
From which everything in the universe comes,
To which everything in the universe returns;
The original nature of your own mind.
The natural state of the universe unmanifest.
Let go into the clear light, trust it, merge with it.
It is your own true nature, it is home.
                                    - The Tibetan Book of the Dead

The Manifesting Magick Bean -

Upon our heightened consciousness, we begin to listen to our desires and revelations of our purpose in life, our awareness and observation of self becomes a precursor of transformation, making changes through empowered choices.

Alongside this may arise the shadows, the doubts - It is fear held in the subconscious and our energetics, ingrained in belief patterns; beliefs that we have no choice, with undertones of victim energy and unworthiness, possibly guilt and shame. If we do not recognise these patterns nor choose to change, for fear of what the fallout maybe, we are resigning ourselves for life to be on repeat, we disempower ourselves!

Your Choice is Your Power — Your Awareness is Your Super Power

Choice is our power, and when we recognise we always have choices, we set an intention and signal to the universe that we are ready for change. For our highest good, that you are worthy of joy, love and peace, your dreams, the relationships etc. This shift is empowered from our hearts in self-love and acceptance.

This message to the Universe by our intention is transmitted and received by our pineal gland. Not only does this amazing little bean in the centre of our mind regulate and heal our bodies, it is also a crystal, a compound of calcite that communicates to our outer world, also found in the labyrinth of the ear, and our bones.

Being a crystal, when the pineal gland is activated through mechanical stress, such as conscious breath work and meditation, it creates an electrical charge which is called piezoelectricity. This energetic charge can also be activated in bone, DNA and various proteins. The word piezoelectricity means electricity resulting from pressure and latent heat.

The crystal piezoelectricity activates our natural energy bio resonance field, which flows within and around us; interacting with the universal field of energy, the universal field of consciousness, which we are all connected to consciously or unconsciously.

When we connect consciously and intentionally, we are flowing with the ocean of opportunities, this is our power and magick!

Our internal world and vibration creates the outer world and our reality, and can be altered by our frequency we choose to resonate. We can consciously retune our subconscious, which is in constant flow with the universal field, to the frequencies we wish to receive and be.

Manifesting is not simply asking, it is also about believing and allowing ourselves to receive. To do this, we must wade the murky depths of our subconscious mind and our unconscious body; to heal our shadows that block us from joy, love and peace; from this life time, our ancestral inheritance and our soul lineage.

Moments of conscious and metaconsciousness states are the boundary to the universal field. They are the check points to ascertain our position and direction of life. It is an opportunity to recalibrate and reset the co-ordinates, to navigate back to our pure essence and purpose, as well as conscious moments of detoxing and healing.

Quite often, we socially project an image as to how we wish to be, or feel we need to be, to be accepted and to belong. We even try hard at the new popular manifesting buzz (a contradiction in itself, as manifestation is about effortlessness, surrendering in trust and allowing the Universe to flow to our highest good). The belief we need to be something to receive something!

This projection of self, creates a vacuum, as it comes from a perception of separation, we are separate to what we desire. This energetic state holds neither substance nor longevity, as this inner conflict exerts huge amounts of energy to try and sustain.

We manifest our dreams when we are already the reality, when our cells physically, emotionally, mentally and spiritually are consistently and coherently vibrating to a higher level of unconditional love, joy and peace. A natural embodiment of inner contentment and gratitude, not forced by what we feel we have to feel, it cannot be cheated!

When we are present in full expression of ourselves held effortlessly in love and acceptance of self, our inner world emanates effortlessly and gracefully to meet the outer world.

Lost fragments of self-realign, our band width and presence expands with definition, the infinite cycle of energy strengthens to a greater sense of wholeness, and we are one, represented by the crown chakra of a thousand petals – Infinite.

> *"I am one with all that is*
> *As Above – So Below*
> *So Within – As Without*
> *Working the Miracles of One – All Miracles Come from One*
> *And So It Is"*

Open Our Hearts
Namaste

I invite you to share your thoughts and pondering, and any aha – realisation moments you may have had.
Include any intentions and action plans that you choose which are in alignment to what you desire:

FURTHER READING

If you have enjoyed learning about the miracle that you are, and wish to know more in how you can be empowered in your health and wellbeing, please go to the online platform, The Infinity Health Hub.

There you will find free articles and membership content with a spectrum of wellbeing awareness, to empower you to make conscious choices of change; including a Sound library of guided meditations and visualisation journeys, as well as the LOVE2Heal online course.

From mental health, money, sexual health, to menopause, no topic will be left uncovered!

YOUR HEALTH IS IN YOUR HANDS

https://www.theinfinityhealthhub.com

REFERENCES

https://warrentonwellness.com/biophotons-the-human-body-emits-communicates-with-and-is-made-from-light/

https://www.thoughtco.com/olfactory-system-4066176

https://chem.libretexts.org/Bookshelves/Physical_and_Theoretical_Chemistry_Textbook_Maps/Supplemental_Modules_(Physical_and_Theoretical_Chemistry)/Quantum_Mechanics/02._Fundamental_Concepts_of_Quantum_Mechanics/Photons

https://courses.lumenlearning.com/boundless-biology/chapter/vision/

https://pubmed.ncbi.nlm.nig.gov/

https://www.ncbi.nlm.nih.gov/pmc/articles/PMC1888599/

https://www.nationalgeographic.com/science/article/photographing-the-glow-of-the-human-body

https://basicmedicalkey.com/the-deep-front-line/
https://www.dunnedwards.com/colors/specs/posts/color-blue-history

https://www.sciencedirect.com/science/article/abs/pii/S1389556721000022

https://www.mdpi.com/2076-3417/10/8/2885

https://www.frontiersin.org/articles/10.3389/fcell.2020.630147/full#:~:text=Approximately%2080%25%20of%20diagnosed%20cases,play%20a%20role%20in%20tumors.

https://www.britannica.com/science/pineal-gland

https://www.goldennumber.net/light-human-body-chakras-golden-ratio/

https://my.clevelandclinic.org/health/articles/22572-serotonin

Pineal gland
https://www.ncbi.nlm.nih.gov/books/NBK550972/

https://brainstuff.org/blog/how-is-serotonin-synthesized-raphe-nucleus

https://www.frontiersin.org/articles/10.3389/fnins.2018.00386/full

ATP deregulation = depression
https://www.google.co.uk/books/edition/The_Role_of_Steroid_Hormones_and_Growth/9yaFEAAAQBAJ?hl=en&gbpv=0

http://www.esalq.usp.br/lepse/imgs/conteudo_thumb/Biophotons.pdf

https://www.medicalnewstoday.com/articles/318652#What-causes-free-radicals-to-develop

Coleys Bacteria to help cancer.

https://www.ncbi.nlm.nih.gov/pmc/articles/PMC1888599/

Melatonin mitochondria
https://www.ncbi.nlm.nih.gov/pmc/articles/PMC5187924/

Eye health blue light exposure
https://eyesafe.com/bluelight/

Fluoride – Glyphosate relationship to pineal gland
https://www.drnorthrup.com/why-you-should-detox-your-pineal-gland/#:~:text=Fluoride%20also%20accumulates%20in%20the,estrogen%2C%20progesterone%2C%20and%20DHEA.

https://www.ncbi.nlm.nih.gov/pmc/articles/PMC3945755/#:~:text=Glyphosate%20disrupts%20the%20balance%20of,and%20Lactobacillus%20are%20especially%20susceptible.

https://www.scirp.org/html/5-3000951_53106.htm

https://www.ncbi.nlm.nih.gov/pmc/articles/PMC5823954/

Glyphosate binding key micro nutrients essential for health.
https://medium.com/@lloydsparks/the-neurophysiology-of-chakras-3f20a0f5b3b5

https://fluoridealert.org/articles/phosphate01/

Mitochondrial Endocrinology
https://www.journals.elsevier.com/molecular-and-cellular-endocrinology

Meditation Studies
https://www.forbes.com/sites/alicegwalton/2015/02/09/7-ways-meditation-can-actually-change-the-brain/?sh=17359c581465

https://news.harvard.edu/gazette/story/2018/04/harvard-researchers-study-how-mindfulness-may-change-the-brain-in-depressed-patients/

https://www.hindawi.com/journals/np/2018/5340717/

Sound Frequency
https://www.to112.com/blogs/news/the-power-of-sound-528hz#:~:text=The%20528%20Hz%20Solfeggio%20Frequency,nature%2C%20and%20the%20divine%20harmony.

https://www.relaxmelodies.com/blog/science-behind-solfeggio-frequencies/

Stress Effect on White Matter
https://news.berkeley.edu/2014/02/11/chronic-stress-predisposes-brain-to-mental-illness/

Sound Frequency and the effects on mind and body
https://www.relaxmelodies.com/blog/science-behind-solfeggio-frequencies/

https://courses.lumenlearning.com/boundless-ap/chapter/distribution-of-spinal-nerves/

https://qbi.uq.edu.au/brain-basics/brain/brain-physiology/what-synaptic-plasticity

Book references-
Healing with Crystals and Chakra Energies- Sue & Simon Lilly

LOVE2Heal

ABOUT THE AUTHOR

Gemma is a healing practitioner with over 15 years of experience in Reiki, Sports and Remedial Massage, and Myofascial Release. Her practice is fueled by a deep reverence for the body's natural ability to heal itself, a journey that has led her to found The Infinity Health Hub and the LOVE2Heal concept. Through these platforms, she aims to empower others in their health and wellness journeys.

Gemma's personal path from self-sabotage to self-love, including her experiences with bulimia and body dysmorphia, deeply influences her approach. She is passionate about helping others overcome limiting beliefs and fears, particularly through her work focused on women's empowerment, which she calls "Pussy Power." She shares her personal and professional insights to help others break free from the blocks that obscure their joy, truth, and inner strength.

With a vision of sustainable, harmonious living on Earth, Gemma also draws on ancient wisdom and sacred traditions to inspire a collective awakening. She envisions a world where we honor our shared humanity and individual uniqueness as part of a greater whole, fostering justice, equality, and inner sovereignty.

Based in East Devon, UK, Gemma resides with her husband, two sons, and their dog. She finds joy in seaside sunrises and moonlight swims, and she connects with her community through The Pyjama Revolution meditation group and her podcast, VOICE, where she advocates for truth, integrity, and compassion.

Printed in Great Britain
by Amazon